LIFE'S LITTLE BIG LESSONS

DR. MARLENA M. CALDWELL ED.D

Copyright © 2019 by Dr. Marlena M. Caldwell Ed.D

ISBN 9781645503767

All rights reserved. No part of this book may be reproduced or transmitted in any form or by any means, electronic or mechanical, including photocopying, recording, or by any information storage and retrieval system, without permission in writing from the copyright owner.

The views expressed in this work are solely those of the author and do not necessarily reflect the views of the publisher, and the publisher hereby disclaims any responsibility for them.

Matchstick Literary
1-888-306-8885
www.matchliterary.com
orders@matchliterary.com

Dedication

This book is dedicated to my family for their on-going, unconditional love and support. Special thanks to Jan who first encouraged me to write about my journey.

Contents

PART ONE
    Chapter 1 Introduction 1
    Chapter 2 Lessons from the Early Years 3
    Chapter 3 Lessons from the Elementary Years................................. 5
    Chapter 4 The Teen Years...10
    Chapter 5 College Years..18
    Chapter 6 Adult Years... 22
    Chapter 7 Niece and Nephew Time 31
    Chapter 8 Swim Program Years..35
    Chapter 9 Illness Years 38
    Life's Little Lessons Master List.. 49

PART TWO
    Never Let Go – David Crowder Band... 56
    Worn – Tenth Avenue North 58
    Lord I Need You – Matt Maher... 59
    Cornerstone – Hillsong Live 61
    Long Way Home – Steven Curtis Chapman 62
    Strong Enough – Matthew West 63
    Even If – Kutless 65
    Busted Heart – For King and Country.. 66
    I Bless Your Name – Selah.. 67
    In Christ Alone – Keith and Kristyn Getty 69
    Promises – Sanctus Real 71
    Where I Belong – Building 429 72
    10,000 Reasons (Bless the Lord) – Matt Redman 73
    Our God – Chris Tomlin...75
    Lay down my Life – Sidewalk Prophets 76
    Lift Me Up – The Afters 77
    Redeemed – Big Daddy Weave... 79
    Only A Mountain – Jason Castro.. 80
    Overcomer – Mandisa 81

Get Down – Audio Adrenaline 83
Through It All – Selah 85
Healing Begins – Tenth Avenue North 87
Speak Life – TobyMac 89
Blessings – Laura Story 91
Dead Man Walking - Jeremy Camp 93
The Champion - Carrie Underwood 94
I'm Gonna Let It Go - Jason Gray.. 95
Scars - I Am They 96
Hope In Front of Me - Danny Gokey 97
Joy - For King and Country 98

Preface

I have been privileged to have many people intersect and influence my life and therefore my experiences as I have traveled the pathway of life. In some ways by reading this book you too will be influenced by their actions, words, and kindness, their guidance and wisdom, as well as their humor. Therefore, I find it critical to introduce you to some of the key characters in my life story.

- Bob and Pat Caldwell – my parents:
    o Myself – Marlena
    o David – My Brother
        - Married Sarah Higgins
            - Ella (niece)
            - Henry (nephew)
    o Jessica – My Sister
        - Married Mitch Hazen
            - Kayla (niece)
            - McKenzie aka Kenzie (niece)
            - Cooper (nephew)

- Lyle and Jan Gibbens – Over time have grown into a set of second parents:
    o Amy – friend and like a sister
        - Married Bryan Beaver
            - Brady
            - Annabelle
            - Brennan
    o Marc – friend and like a brother
        - Married Marci Klayder
            - Adele
            - Blair
            - Callan

This book is a collection of stories, adventures, and journeys I have had throughout my life time and the lessons I have learned from each. At times in some chapters the stories build on each other however, most often each story or example or journey are exclusive and unique.

PART ONE

INTRODUCTION

"Life is not easy for any of us. But what of that? We must have perseverance and above all confidence in ourselves. We must believe that we are gifted for something and that this thing must be attained."

Marie Curie

Curie lived from 1867-1934 and was most known for her work in the scientific fields of physics and chemistry. Her scientific work won her not just one, but two Nobel Prizes in multiple science areas. She was the first woman to win a Nobel Prize, is the only woman to have won two, and is the only person to have won two in multiple areas of science. Much of her work focused on research in radioactivity including its use in x-rays. During World War I she provided service in using portable x-rays, which she invented. She died at age sixty-seven from Aplastic Anemia brought on by exposure to radiation, most likely much of which occurred during her military service.

Marie Curie is an inspiration of what we can do with our gifts and talents when we put our minds to making something from nothing. Her work and service embody perseverance. Thinking about the obstacles and stereotypes of her time period that she was able to overcome are amazing and inspirational.

I was drawn to this quote by Curie for two reasons. The first being that of sentence one; "Life is not easy for any of us." When we are faced with difficult circumstances or tragedy it is often easy to get caught in our one spinning place, feeling alone and stuck. This sentence reminds me that all of us face difficulty, sadness, and loneliness in our lives. You will find upon reading further some of the difficult situations I have faced in my lifetime and the lessons I have learned by experiencing the worst life has to offer.

Yet I am still standing and still here writing because of the second part of this quote the perseverance and confidence to use my gifts. I would even expand on this further to say perseverance and confidence provided through my relationship with God to use my gifts, talents, and circumstances to glorify Him. To persevere, to overcome, these are the traits which lead to the confidence we gain going through life. Difficult circumstances require perseverance but produce confidence as we journey on the road of life.

The connections you make to your own life and circumstances as you read the following pages is the reason for this book. Whether you laugh, cry, are shocked, or awed the bottom line is the confidence we gain going through life's activities and hardships. The lesson's God has taught us and the ways in which we use these "gifts" to help others. My prayer is that something in my thoughts, actions, or experiences would resonate in your very heart to produce the perseverance to fight the good and honorable fight another day. To use your gifts, through hard work, in leadership and service to others as you glorify our Lord and Savior, Jesus Christ.

Chapter 2
Lessons from the Early Years

As a young toddler I enjoyed being in the walker. For those of you wondering what a walker is it is this contraption thing which a young child can sit in as they are learning to walk. It supports the child but allows him or her to push around with their feet to move. The entire piece is on wheels so it glides easily on smooth surfaces. We had just moved to Cincinnati, Ohio and while waiting for the purchase of our house, my parents and I lived upstairs in my Mom's Sister's old farm house. With all wood floors it was an amazing place to cruise in my walker. While happily cruising around one day there was the opportunity for a new adventure and all that could be heard in the house was a clunk, clunk, clunk…My Aunt who was downstairs began yelling my Dad's name and my Dad who was upstairs began feeling very ill. Life's Little Lesson– If there is an open door…go through it!

As parents of a toddler, my Mom and Dad were ready for a break after putting me in the crib for the night. They settled me in, tucked the blanket, kissed my head, said goodnight, and turned off the lights. With a sigh after a long day they settled in for some adult conversation and T.V. Their adult time was quickly interrupted by a wandering, little toddler. Somewhat perplexed as to how I made it out of the crib and into the living room, my parents swept me up, tucked me back in the crib. However, my parents were on to me and they stood at the door and watched as I totally climb from the crib onto the top of the chest of drawers, down the front of the furniture using the drawer edges as a ledge and onto the floor. My secret was out and the furniture was moved. Life's Little Lesson – Be creative in finding solutions to the problems you face.

Many of my earliest memories are of family. I can recall feeling like such a big kid getting to ride in a company truck with my Grandpa and Dad as they would go out to potential clients and bid fence jobs. My Grandpa was a business owner and started the Cherry Grove Fence Company which installed all different types of fences. My Grandpa also loved the Cincinnati Reds and I have vague memories of attending a game again with my Grandpa and Dad. We sat way up in the nosebleed section but I remember a feeling of excitement for my first baseball game. Additionally, I have memories of eating out at our favorite restaurant called the Log Cabin. I remember getting ham every time we went there with my parents and grand-parents. Unfortunately, I also have the memory of the day my Grandpa passed away. I have the memories of my Dad performing CPR, lots of what felt like chaos and movement all around me, and crying. Life's Little Lesson – Family plays such an important part in our memories.

Another one of my most favorite memories was while we lived in Ohio we had family friends and the four of us me, David, and their two boys Mike and Jeff used to play together for hours. Our most favorite activity…the sit and spin. Not only would we have competitions as to who could last the longest but we experimented with various ways to spin, how many people could spin at once, and what items we could keep spinning the longest. We also loved to jump on the furniture and make up games like there were killer alligators on the floor and you couldn't touch the floor so we would jump from furniture piece to piece. We were always doing something with them. Our last evening together before we moved to Kansas was like any normal play time together. We jumped on furniture, ran around outside, played on the sit and spin, and argued. Everyday normal activities but how life was about to change. Mike and Jeff were my best friends and we were moving halfway across the United States away from them. Life's Little Lessons – Goodbyes are hard on everyone.

Chapter 3
Lessons from the Elementary Years

When we first moved to Kansas in 1980 my Dad was teaching at MidAmerica Nazarene University and he had an office in the basement of the boy's dorm. My brother and I often spent time with Dad there and on one particular occasion were both in the narrow hallway leading to his office and decided to race. Upon take off it was a close race. I had my eye on the finish line while David was in maximum drive focused on moving his feet looking at the ground. Needless to say he did not see the phone booth sticking out from the wall. Before I could say anything or take evasive measures, he smacked his head directly into the wooden panel sticking out from the wall. After a minute of trying to process what had happened he saw blood dripping from his hand which had come from his head and he started yelling, "Emergency, Emergency, call an ambulance." My Dad took him for stitches and that was the end of our racing career in the basement of Lampher. Life's Little Lesson - This was a painful life lesson for my Brother but we both learned to look up when you are racing down a hallway, you never know what could be sticking out of the wall.

The bell rang for us to go to recess and I followed a group of second graders who looked like they knew what they were doing. It was my first day in second grade, in a new school, in a new state. I watched as they began to walk across the parallel bars and jump to a single cross bar about two feet away. Building my courage I entered the waiting line. At my turn, I boldly climbed and balanced on the bars, began the balanced walk to the end and just as I started to jump my foot slipped off the metal bar and I did a faceplant on the gravel playground. Being the tough kid I was I just picked myself up brushed myself off, rubbed my aching nose and ran off to try something less gymnastics and more sporty with a ball. Having figured out to avoid the metal equipment area second recess was going much smoother until the whistle came for line up. Everyone made a mad dash for the class lines and just as I arrived at my line so did another kid and the two of us smacked heads. When we got inside my teacher sent me to the office to see the nurse, however, when I asked if the nurse was there the office staff said no and I just turned around and went back to class. My parents were somewhat traumatized when I walked in after school with a swollen nose and a bouncy ball sized knot just above my left eye. Life's Little Lesson – The playground can be a tough place even when you are following the examples and rules.

It was during an elementary children's church service in which I decided to give my life to Jesus and ask Him to come into my heart. For a kid that is some pretty big theology so I waited until we got home that Sunday and I told my parents what I wanted to do. Looking back on it I am sure it was one of their most exciting moments as they led me in the prayer of salvation in our living room and talked to me further about what it meant to be a follower of Christ. Life's Little Lesson – Big moments in life should be shared with family.

As most neighborhoods do we had a bully. He roamed the streets looking for trouble and kids to torment. I happened to have two significant run ins with this particular bully. The first began with my best friend and I finding a bird's nest with robin eggs in it. The neighborhood bully felt strongly it was his responsibility to destroy the eggs while my friend and I were determined to save the tiny, helpless eggs. We grabbed the eggs seconds before being crushed in a single blow and took off running. We dodged in and out of trees, across the stream, and headed down the street toward safety. With the bully hot on our trail we entered the safety zone, my best friend's house, as we made it to his porch and into the front door we realized that in our attempt to flee the bully, dashing in and out of houses, around shrubs and trees, in the midst of our attempt to save the eggs we had each unintentionally squished the eggs in our hands while running. Life's Little Lesson – don't run with eggs in your hand.

My second run in with this young man came as we walked home from school on a sunny, warm afternoon. Third grade was the magic grade. The grade when you could start riding your bike to school. I was in 6th grade but my brother had hit third and it was a joy for him to get to ride his bike. This particular day the bully was on his bike and David (my brother) was on his. The bully began taunting David and running his front tire into David's back tire. I properly warned our bully to stop but he was not heeding the warning. In order to save my brother from what I knew was going to be a crash and injury I ran up behind the bully grabbed his shirt and pulled him off his bike. Simultaneously, I yelled "I told you to leave him alone." Befuddled as to how he got to the ground, the bully quickly recovered to his feet and determined revenge was required. I calmly suggested not fighting but it was happening. Somewhat like the Spiderman movie I dodged a fist headed toward my face and returned a fistful of happiness to the bully's nose. Then I told David to get home and I took off running as fast as I could all the way to our house. We dodged inside the garage and looked back to see if we were pursued. No pursuit ensued but I did notice the following day our seats had been separated at school. Life's Little Lesson – always stick up for family but not necessarily through fighting.

I was in kindergarten when I began playing soccer. As a small child in Ohio, I can remember the field area we played on and a feeling of enjoyment as we learned to dribble, pass and kick. Soccer in Kansas was not as popular at the time of our move but I did get to play on a coed team with mostly boys in 2nd through 4th grade. The sport was gaining popularity and we had enough interest to begin leagues devoted just for girls so I switched to an all girls team. By 6th grade I was quite the competitive soccer player. I loved playing and not only had I started playing the goalkeeper position but I played all the time. My Brother and I, neighborhood kids, and even teammates would play anytime we could in the backyard, at recess, meeting at the school field on a Saturday. It didn't matter the size or shape, if we could make a field we played. In fact, we were once playing a competitive game with the neighborhood kids in our front yard and broke the kitchen bay window with a game winning goal and that became the final game in the front yard. Moving the game to the driveway with a perfect size goal at the garage door was not an improvement. I spent any allowance I earned and many birthday dollars paying for broken garage door windows. It got to where my Dad just said his name at the glass shop and they knew what he needed. One of our all time favorite fields was the indoor field we created in the finished basement family room. With furniture lining the outside, this room made a perfect oval for an indoor soccer field. We stuffed pillows under the spaces in the couch and chairs; we found boxes to fill in a few gaps and left the space for the goals at each end open. Kansas City had a popular indoor soccer team called the Comets at this time and they had a spectacular introduction for the players and to the game. My bedroom was next to this family room so I would jump on my bed read the introduction for the game, which I had on a poster, and we would play. We played for hours like that and would literally be dripping with sweat when we stopped for a break. We used a small size 2 ball which we got at a comets game or a stuffed size 4 ball. Size of the ball is only important when you think about the hours we devoted to playing and the footwork we developed by playing with such a small ball in close quarters. Life's Little Lesson – when you find something you love and you devote time to learning it well; you never know where it will take you.

Speaking of close quarters, my Mom would sometimes decorate this family room and Christmas time was one of the major times we had decorations throughout the house and family room. Sitting on one of the end tables was the cute family of Christmas mice. These were fancy figurines dress in Christmas attire and one was even a bell. You know where this is headed and you would be right, in one of our all out, sacrifice your body, competitive indoor games we broke the mouse bell. It was nailed by the ball and upon falling to the second layer of table broke into several pieces. The game naturally came to a halt as we now had to problem solve telling mom or fixing it. David, being a model car enthusiast, had super glue in his room. He casually roamed upstairs and into his room. Got the glue and made it back down undetected. We put the pieces back together like a jigsaw puzzle and super glued it the best we could. There was a sliver of mouse missing and the bell never quite rang right but we put it back on the table with the mice family. Our repair job remained unnoticed until Mom went to pack up the Christmas decorations and she came to the family of mice. Lucky for us there was no financial penalty and I think Mom kind of thought it was ingenious of us to try to fix it that we didn't even get in trouble. Life's Little Lesson – if you break it…fix it, no matter the cost.

After finishing a girl scout meeting at my elementary school, my friends and I all walked out of the building together. We said our goodbyes and headed toward our respective cars. One of my friends was still waiting so my Mom and I offered her a ride. She hopped in the front, I slid in the back, and Mom was just about ready to drive off as my friend's Mom arrived. She quickly changed cars as our Moms had a conversation. As they were talking I slid by my Mom standing in the driver's side door and re-entered the car scooting my way across the front seat to the passenger side. A few minutes of adult conversation and then we were on our way home. As my Mom gently turned the corner of the school parking lot the passenger side door swung open and before either of us knew what was happening I had fallen out of the car, hit the pavement in what was a back roll type tuck and bounced back to my feet. Mom was out of the car and screaming at me only seconds after my abrupt exit from the car. Her screaming was fear and panic not anger but to her and my delight I was standing there unharmed. Shaken, frightened but no injuries to report. We climbed back in the car and finished the three minute drive home. In analyzing the situation, it became clear that when my friend exited our car to get into her car the passenger side door was not properly and fully closed therefore when I entered from the driver's side door the problem was not corrected leading to my unexpected departure from the car moments later as we turned and the door flew open. Life's Little Lesson - The seatbelt law! Obey it.

One of the best field trips I recall as an elementary student was the one to Exchange City. Part of the excitement was because of the preparation we did for the trip. We learned about city government, elections, leadership, store ownership, how to fill out a job application, calculating a checkbook, and writing checks. The paper came which described all the jobs at Exchange City and we were to discuss with our parents the various jobs and then determine our top three. The following day we completed an application process for our number one job choice. Elections were held for the position of Mayor, everyone else received a paper with their job name on it and the exciting day came. I was assigned to the sign shop. Our business earned money by making the title signs for all the other shops and buildings as well as painting small ceramic picture frames and figurines which we sold throughout the day. For a fifth grader this was the coolest place… a miniature city under one roof. On your breaks from work you had to deposit your pay checks and then you could write checks for things you wanted to buy from the other stores or if you were fined for running, walking on the grass, or other violations. Life's Little Lesson – Your very first job says a lot about what you enjoy and skills which God has gifted to you. My example the sign shop required creativity, organization, and follow through.

Chapter 4
The Teen Years

I also developed a love for soccer juggling. Basically you can use any part of your body except for hands to keep the ball in the air and you see how many times you can kick or bounce the ball or how long you can keep the ball in the air. Challenging myself to a juggling contest meant that I could play soccer even when there were no teammates or neighborhood games to be played. This form of soccer and kicking the ball off of our brick house was my entertainment during the gulf war. Since that was all that was on TV for night after night I turned the porch light on the patio and would juggle or bounce the ball off the house for hours. Not sure looking back my parents enjoyed the thud against the house night after night, hour after hour, but nonetheless they let me play. Life's Little Lesson – Make goals and then challenge yourself to break them.

There is a five year difference in age between myself and my younger sister, Jessica. One day when I was in junior high and she was a young elementary student she came and asked if she could spend the night at my house. Totally confused at first I then realized she meant to spend the night in my room. Any time from then on we have talked about spending the night it has always been, "Spend the night at your house." Life's Little Lesson – I enjoyed having an Open "House" Policy.

We moved to an Olathe neighborhood which was located on a hill and only had about fifteen homes. Each home sat on about two acres of land and the entire neighborhood was surrounded by wooded areas on three sides. In 1972 a tornado had ripped through the neighborhood and destroyed many of the homes. Having been rebuilt in was a nice place to live with many outdoor activities as options for curious children. The three of us along with a few neighborhood children enjoyed exploring the woods around our houses and searching for treasure. The woods held all kinds of household, garage, and other items which were blown away during the tornado. We found kitchen appliances, bottles of all sorts, and even a car. These adventures for treasure provided hours of fun and entertainment and we never came back without a story of something we found. Life's Little Lesson – There is treasure all around us, sometimes it is just covered by dirt.

Sitting on two acres of land, we owned a riding lawn mower in order to cut the majority of the grass. I had a lesson in driving the riding mower and had cut part of the grass. Things were going great until my Father had me pull into the garage to park the mower. Jessica had joined me on the back of the seat for a ride into the garage and we joyfully rode along. With my Father leading me, I came to the spot in the garage to park the mower. Instead of parking by pushing on the brake I mistakenly pushed the gas and ran right into my Dad pushing him into the wall of the garage and house. The wall board gave way with the force of the crash and there was a butt and back hole in the wall from the force at which I had crashed into and pushed my Dad. Luckily for me and him there were only minor injuries. I tried my best to blame the accident on Jessica because she was riding on back with me but no one to this day will believe it. Life's Little Lesson – There are moments in life which need to be caught on video in order to win $10,000.

My siblings and I talked our parents into taking us for a day of fun in the sun at our local water park. There were various water slides, pools, a lagoon type lake area, and a wave pool. Water people would totally describe my brother, sister, and I but not so much of a description for our parents. I know they could save themselves had they ever gotten into trouble in the water but love of the water would not have been their mantra ever. They made sure we could swim and enjoy the water since it had not been something encouraged or forced upon them. We even had a pool in our backyard for all of my junior high, high school, college, and into my adult years. Needless to say there was some hesitation around water when it came to my Mother and Father. In part of the lake area at the water park was a section where you could take out a kayak or paddle boat. I begged and begged until finally my father gave in and we decided to do the paddle boat. Little did I know the entire time we were out on the water my father was trembling in fear, although we both were wearing life jackets. Life's Little Lesson – Parents sometimes do things for their children they would have never tried on their own.

My club soccer team the KC Wildcats consisted of teammates from all of the Kansas City area. We were a select team meaning you had to try out for the team every year in late summer. We were a traveling team and traveled to tournaments all across the Midwest and U.S. In our league play there were very few teams in our age group who played competitive soccer so we often played up in the Under 19 division. The skill and competition greatly impacted my team's ability to play at higher levels and develop the fundamentals of the game faster playing against such competitive teams. Therefore, we enjoyed great success when playing against teams of our own age in tournaments. We were Kansas State Cup champions six years straight during our time with the core returning players. We participated in tournaments in Oklahoma, South Dakota, Indiana, Nebraska, Iowa, Missouri, Colorado, New York, and probably a few I missed. There are several tournaments that stand out either because of our success as a team, or my success as a goalkeeper, or because of our team activities while on the road. I could highlight things like late night soccer games in hotel hallways, or hairspray match lighting science experiments, various movie adventures, to a twenty-five hour train ride or maybe on the field side of things the hot, dreadful fields of sun-scorched Oklahoma to the lush, beauty of playing at the Air Force Academy. There is also the success of making it to the finals of the Junior Olympics in New York, winning the regional tournament, to being named most valuable player of the tournament. Life's Little Lesson – Play Hard! No matter what you are doing! Success and fun are bound to be a part, if you are giving all you have!

MacGyver Mondays became a tradition I looked forward to every week while I was in junior high school and high school. On Mondays I watched Amy and Marc while Lyle and Jan went to music rehearsal at church for their small group. I would even come a half hour early just so we could start the show at 7:00pm. MacGyver was a genius when it came to making something from nothing and he worked to solve problems. Somewhat as a government agent his job on the T.V. show took him around the world to rescue people, save government top secrets, and solve humanitarian problems. Life's Little Lesson – You can make just about anything out of some string, a gum wrapper, and tape.

Located just about an hour away is the theme park called Worlds of Fun. As a teenager I managed to go at least once a year with either a church group, a friend group, or occasionally with my family. A group of us from my high school soccer team decided to surprise our friend with a special birthday lunch and an afternoon/evening of rides, roller coasters, and games at the park. After a nice lunch we headed to the park. Our first adventure ride was the tram headed into the park entrance. It was on this tram ride that I noticed my shoe had come untied and I needed to tie my shoe. I placed my ticket in my mouth and proceeded to begin tying my shoe. One of my friends asked me a question and without thinking I opened my mouth to answer. The gusting Kansas wind picked up the ticket right off my lips and it was blowing away. Simultaneously as the gusty breeze lifted the ticket I sprang from my seat and launched myself onto the cement headed in the direction of my flying ticket. My moving body disembarked the tram to the solid, still ground and made for an interesting landing which I managed to not completely face plant but still had to jump up off the ground to retrieve my floating ticket. To my total embarrassment the tram had come to a full and complete stop and was there waiting for my return. As I jogged back and jumped onto the tram, the attendant with the microphone said, "We could have stopped, you know." How would I have known that information and really what I did was total reaction. It is not like I thought about what I was doing, I just did it. Life's Little Lesson - Never, never put important tickets in your mouth.

On another occasion I went to Worlds of Fun with my family. We had a great day riding rides, eating junk food, playing games, and being together. It was getting later in the afternoon and we were about to head out of the park when Jessica, my sister, decided she needed something from the gift shop with the money she still had. David and I decided to hop on a ride close to the gift shop so they could shop and we could ride. In the meantime, it had started a gentle rain and the park was beginning to clear out. We jumped on this whirl-a-tilt type ride and started going around in circles, then each car while still moving in a circle kind of moved in and out so you felt like you were going up and down hills. The ride ended and Mom, Dad, Jessica were still in the gift shop so David and I ran around to enter the gate again for a second ride. During this ride the rain picked up but we were having fun. So the ride operator let us keep going. We noticed they were ready to go and gave the signal to shut down. Getting off the ride in the now pouring rain we were soaked. By the time we made it to the car no one was dry but you could ring the water out of David and my clothes. Life's Little Lesson – Sometimes just embrace and go for playing in the pouring rain.

From my freshman to my senior year I had started every varsity soccer game on the schedule. I had played through illness and some minor injuries but in what was going to be the last game of my high school soccer career I was faced with a huge dilemma. Play with what was a full lower leg hematoma (my entire lower leg, shin and calf was bruised) and risk further injury with possible loss of a soccer scholarship or sit out the final game. Life's Little Lesson – Some decisions are better left to your parents and you just follow their lead.

We grew up near a community lake. This lake was large enough for small fishing boats, canoes, kayaks, and at times has allowed swimming in a man-made beach area. There are picnic areas and a lake golf course just to the East of the water. To allow for overflow during snow and rain, the lake has a spillway and flatland area. In certain times of the year the spillway can become flooded or overflowing with water and cause an entrance to the park to flood as well. Often a park ranger would close off this entrance in order to avoid vehicles from getting stuck in the flowing water or washed down-stream in the fast-flowing creek. On one rainy, Spring night my brother and I were headed home from an event in separate cars. He was in a small, two door Ford escort and I followed in a Chevy S-10 Pickup. David was in the lead and took the short-cut through the lake road. By now it had been raining non-stop for most of the day and there was water flowing through the spillway and over the road. However, the park ranger had not been there yet to close the road and David proceeded to enter the water and make his way through to the other side. This is where women's intuition kicked in, and for a moment I thought this is a bad idea, but like most siblings I couldn't let my brother go through and me not get over there especially driving a pickup truck. S-10s are small trucks but in my mind it was a truck nonetheless. So I quickly followed in his path, entering the water at a fairly good pace in order to make it through, however my adventure through the flowing water was not so smooth. The truck died right in the middle of the spillway with water flowing fast underneath and rising by the minute. When I stepped out of the truck the fast moving water easily covered my shoe and no matter what we tried the truck would not start. I stayed with the truck and my Brother drove the few minutes home. As he entered the house he yelled, "Get a rope, we have to pull Marlena's truck out of the creek." Dad was like what is going on, why is she in the creek? They made it back just in time for the park ranger to show up to close the gates allowing no one to cross the now shin deep cold, fast-moving water. The ranger assisted us in calling for a tow truck and my truck was safely pulled out of the water and thank goodness insurance covered all but the deductible of a new engine. Life's Little Lesson - If your gut is telling you something LISTEN to it.

    My Sister, Jessica and I decided to take this huge, heavy, metal canoe for a day of canoeing on the lake. We had our oars, the cooler, and lifejackets. We were well prepared for a day in the canoe. As water safety instructors (WSI) we were well trained for water activities. I was excited to get on the water and begin our adventure. We pushed off from the boat ramp and paddled three or four strokes. Our father, who had helped us get it out of the truck and into the water, was just then walking back to his car to leave. Mine and Jessica's paddling had taken us directly into the path of a fishing boat. We tried everything to steer the canoe away from the fishing boat but we were heading straight into a collision. My problem solving, quick action section of my brain took over and before I even really explained to Jessica, I stood up, stepped on the side, and pushed off into the water yelling, "I'm jumping in to stop this thing!" All I could hear as my head fell under the water was NOOOO! Then as I popped out of the water I grabbed the canoe to get it stopped which by then was sitting upside down and Jessica was coming up from under the water. Our Dad saw the entire event from the car and turned around to come back. Good thing too because our canoeing adventure was over. As I jumped and Jessica did not she was caught by the tipping canoe and nailed by the heavy, metal side on her thigh. Life's Little Lesson - When someone in the canoe decides to bail you best decide quickly to jump with them.

I met my best friend in high school on our first day of our sophomore year. We ended up having several classes together including history and physical education. While I was the out-going, hard-core athlete; he was the cool headed, hard-working actor/singer. Although we were so very opposite in many ways we hit it off and our friendship grew over our three years in high school. We became pretty inseparable and invaluable to each other as a source of support, help, competition, and friendship. I became a theatre/ performance fan and he found my sports to be an exciting cheering opportunity. We enjoyed a variety of normal teen activities as well as attending various sporting and theatre events in our community. We were the best of friends and high school ended with each of us going separate ways but wanting to keep in touch. Life's Little Lesson – When you find a best friend nurture the relationship.

My high school soccer team was in the race for a number one seed in post season play and our coach was very passionate about our efforts on and off the field. He held very high standards for us as both students and athletes. I appreciated Coach Hair's intensity and passion because I was as equally passionate and competitive as a player. Maybe not so much as a student, much to the disapproval of my educator parents, but definitely as a soccer player. As the goalkeeper of my high school team I provided leadership to the defense and support to our offense. We had a series of plays designed for various situations and one of those was a tricky play on an inbounds kick or goal kick. I would run outside the eighteen yard box and my defender would pass me the ball. At that time I would receive the ball just outside the box, tap it back inside the box and then pick it up for a long punt. On this particular occasion we decided to try the play and I took off running to the outside, the pass came to me at a slower pace and by the time the ball got there an opposing player was bearing down on me. They expected me to try to touch the ball back in the box so instead I turned to the outside of the field and dribbled forward. I had space so I dribbled. As another opposing player approached I thought briefly about passing the ball but instead made a head fake and went right around the second player. At this point I was fairly close to midfield, I could hear Coach Hair yelling something at me and there were players beginning to merge into my path so I launched the ball to our offense. After the kick my eye caught that of coach's and as I ran back to the goal he ran with me on the sideline yelling the entire way. His comments were not that of approval of my recent actions. When I got back in the box and our offense had the ball at the other end, I looked over at his ranting and raving self and told him to "calm down, everything is okay." Life's Little Lesson – When you make the right decision stick with it no matter what anyone says.

As a senior in high school I was fortunate to have Mr. Ralph Dennis for a semester of an elective psychology class. He was a legend in the school for being an amazing teacher and coach. I was not disappointed either. He was amazing. There were rules and expectations, procedures and routines but students, like me, who followed most directions and enjoyed the interaction of activities, did quite well in his class and developed a positive student-teacher relationship. I am not sure really anyone did poorly because he made you want to succeed. After our lessons and exams we had the opportunity to learn to juggle. Yes, I said juggle, like a circus clown, in his class after our work was done. He even led sessions teaching the technique or showing an advanced skill of juggling. He said that we had enough pressures as seniors and he was going to help take some of it off. I loved even five minutes of juggling time. It made such a difference in my day. Life's Little Lesson – Sometimes when the pressure is on you just have to stop and juggle.

Baptism in the Church of the Nazarene signifies to the outside world the change that has happened in your heart and that you are committing your life and the rest of your days to God. You are going to follow His direction and be a light for others. Mom, David, Jessica, and I were all baptized in a river in my Dad's home state of Alabama. The congregation in the church he had grown up in was present and participated in the celebration. Life's Little Lesson – My Dad is proof that good things can come from Alabama besides football.

Choosing a college was a difficult task. I was a competitive athlete and wanted to play soccer at the college level. It was a joy and honor to be recruited by some of the best division 1 schools, interested in having me talk with them about attending school and playing soccer. Amazing schools like the University of Cincinnati, University of Alabama, and my personal favorite, Yale University sent recruitment information and contact numbers. In the end, I was drawn to a smaller school where I could play immediately and make a difference from the beginning of my freshman year. During this decision making time my Mom gave me a bible verse to keep and focus on as I tried to make this choice. The verse is Psalms 84:11 "For the Lord God is a sun and shield; The Lord gives grace and glory; No good thing does He withhold from those who walk uprightly" (NASB, 2012). I was so conflicted during this decision making opportunity that I wondered where God was in all of it and questioned how to process His plan. Looking back I think that was my Mother's plan for the verse. To help me to see that if I gave my questions to God, gave my future to God and worked to walk uprightly, God's hand would be in the plan. Also that through His grace and glory I would sense the right steps to follow in making the critical choices which defined my career and various other opportunities. Life's Little Lesson – seek first knowing and glorifying God.

Chapter 5
College Years

After being heavily recruited by several colleges and universities, I settled on a small NAIA school where I was eager to begin classes in my degree area and play soccer as a starting goalkeeper for the women's team. To my disappointment both the women's and men's teams were coached by the same person and our seasons, practices, and work out schedules were the same. Not that I have ever had a problem playing soccer or working out with boy soccer players but little attention was given to the women's team. We were being led by senior girls who knew more about the next party than they did about soccer. Needless to say I was a bit distraught... teammates breaking all kinds of rules, traveling a distance to another university for an evening of partying, and then there was the lack of focus on both soccer and school. These were the two things I was most passionate about. When the first Sunday rolled around and I absolutely forced myself to go to church, I realized that although soccer had been such a huge and important part of my life it was not worth this. This being the turmoil on the team, the lack of direction and leadership, the partying, and the struggle to go to church. As hard a decisions as it was to make a college choice the decision to call my parents and explain the situation was just as difficult. I knew they would be very supportive and talk through the situation with me and ultimately support what I needed at the time. However, there were all those people watching my soccer career with anticipation, one of the main ones being my high school soccer coach. What would they think and how could I ever truly explain the terrible situation I had entered. I thought to myself, as I reflected on the hoopla around getting a soccer scholarship, making the college decision and God's plan for my life. I debated with myself about giving up on soccer because my two options for school now neither one offered women's soccer at the time of my college career. To this point in my life it was the roughest forty-eight hours as I waited for my parents to arrive, pack my stuff, and return to "sweet home sweet" as my nephew Cooper says. Life's Little Lesson – You cannot be worried about what other people think when God is clearly sending you a message. In my case, at this time in my life, soccer was not as important as my emotional and spiritual health.

I returned to my hometown, church affiliated college and enrolled just in time for classes to start. I missed much of orientation but was very familiar with the campus and many staff since this is where my Dad had taught. In fact, many classes that first semester began with Marlena Caldwell...wow, nice to have you here, how is your Dad or I remember you as a small child running around here following your Dad. School was great and classes that semester were awesome. I was so motivated to do well and learn it was exciting to be doing things focused on education and teaching physical education/health. Although I had not participated on a track team since my eighth grade year of junior high school, I was a walk-on athlete for the fall and winter indoor college track seasons my freshman year. In the spring of my freshman year I was fortunate to get hired as a Rule 10 high school girl's soccer coach at Shawnee Mission North High School. The moment I started coaching I saw the picture develop in my mind and I never looked back. Coaching became a passion and in one form or another I have continued a coaching role ever since. I coached soccer for three years while in college and only quit in order to do my student teaching in the spring of my senior year. I also began coaching seventh grade girl's junior high volleyball and basketball in Bonner Springs as a Rule 10 coach. I was very blessed to have had those coaching opportunities while in college and that each role related directly to my career path. Life's Little Lesson – Sometimes prayers are answered with new opportunities which allow us to see gifts and interests we never knew we had.

When I was in eighth grade I met Lyle and Jan and their two children, Amy and Marc. Lyle was a teacher in the local school district and Jan stayed home with the children. As I got to know them better and them me, I started watching the children when they would run errands and for Monday nights when they had music rehearsal for the group they sang in at church. Our friendship developed and after many years I have become part of the family. When Marc entered school several years after I met them, Jan decided to return to teaching school as well. It was my junior year in college when Lyle became very ill. His journey included major surgery, fifty-five days in a coma, and rehab. Eventually diagnosed with Hemolytic Anemia, it was a very rough journey with many ups and downs. There were times during the fifty-five days that Jan would call and have me bring the kids down to the hospital because they were not sure Lyle was going to make it. Then there were the nights alone in the house with the kids when Jan would come in for a few hours of rest and would say, "Mar, I don't think he is going to make it." I knew the fear and worry of her heart as she lay there trying to rest but thinking of a difficult future. My heart ached in those days and times; I questioned God's will and felt utterly helpless in relieving any of the stress, worry, and fears. Lyle's time of rehab was my most difficult time with his illness journey. His vocal cords were paralyzed so he talked in a raspy whisper, which I found very difficult to understand, he was frail with little muscle mass, and even the smallest of tasks wore him out. From the marathon runner, bike riding, athlete to the guy laying in the bed; frustrated and angered me. I questioned why he and they as a family had to endure such hardship. I was angry with God and it was difficult to force myself to go and see him during the recovery phase. Not that I didn't want to see him and support him but at how angry I felt. The following summer, the five of us took several trips together and in each one I saw Lyle's strength returning little by little. One of our trips was to visit our friends who introduced me to Lyle and Jan. It was a great trip but while there we passed around the stomach flu… the tilt-a-whirl scene in the movie Sandlot took on a whole new meaning for us that summer. Life's Little Lesson – God really can use all circumstances to glorify Him.

Now let us catch back up with my best friend from high school. When I returned home and went to enroll for college he decided to enroll also as an elementary education major. He had talked about being a teacher and maybe even a principal one day. So we began college together. Our friendship remained strong and probably even grew stronger as we spent numerous hours together on campus, in classes, studying, and enjoying life together. Somewhere along the line my feelings for him shifted from friendship to something a little more and I dreamed of the day we would marry. He was after all my best friend. It was the end of summer, just before we were to return to classes and we had a talk. Friends or more than friends…I expressed my appreciation and admiration of him, I discussed our friendship and our likes and dislikes, I told him I loved him. In return, I received some expressions of friendship, things he valued about our relationship but not much else. Feeling slightly embarrassed I quickly said I knew that was a lot to take in and it may need some time to digest and think about. We went our separate ways and did not really speak again. I was sad that there was no real response to my open heart but then a week or two into classes I received an early, Saturday morning phone call telling me that he had been arrested and there was an article in the paper. Our advisor and friend did not want me to see it, read about it, or hear it from someone else so she called. Life's Little Lesson – Sometimes God doesn't just close a door, he slams it.

As I finished my student teaching experience I had the opportunity to coach track at Robert E. Clark Middle School in Bonner Springs, Kansas.

During my college years I was fortunate to use the Kansas Rule 10 coaching guidelines in order to coach high school girls soccer, 7th grade volleyball, 7th grade basketball and 7-9 track. With a certified teacher traveling with us, I was able to coach and participate as a staff member as I earned my education degree. It was toward the final days of my student teaching and one of the final track meets of the season. We were just north of our district at a neighboring school for a track meet and I suddenly became very ill. In the restroom I felt very faint, sick to my stomach and terrible pain in my lower back on the right side. I knew I couldn't even return to the field so I sent a message with one of the students to let my cooperating teacher know I was sick and going home. As I drove the 40 or so minutes it became increasingly difficult to dismiss the pain in my lower back which was now beginning to wrap around to my lower abdomen as well as to keep my stomach contents in my stomach. I turned at the stoplight on Highway 7 and Santa Fe just three miles from home and began throwing up as I was driving. Racing home and into the driveway, I pulled my shirt off careful not to spill on my car, let the shirt fall to the ground, left the car door open and ran to the front door of the house. All that to find the door locked. I rang the bell, knocked on the door until my Mom came in hollering about me and my key. I pushed my way in and managed to yell, "I'm dying, and this is it." Then I threw up again. I rolled around on my bed trying to explain what was wrong and how this all started and again I thought this is the end, Lord Jesus here I come. However, my Mother had a suspicion she knew what it was and we were off to the emergency room. After some morphine and a few tests, they determined I had a kidney stone which was stuck in the urinary tract causing extreme pain and things to back up which for me led to the throwing up. The next morning I had a surgery to remove the stone and place a stint in order for things to work even through the swelling and pain. I missed the remainder of my student teaching days but was feeling better by graduation. Life's Little Lesson - Sometimes it is extremely helpful to be wearing two shirts.

    College graduation was a true celebration since only weeks earlier, I thought I was dying and Lyle who truly was at heaven's doorstep was here to celebrate with us. At high school graduation I skipped out on the open house but for college graduation we had a small gathering of family, close friends, and some of the teachers I had worked with while coaching and student teaching. It was a very fun and relaxing way to celebrate a major accomplishment. Life's Little Lesson – Little celebrations are great ways to thank those people who have made a difference in your life.

CHAPTER 6
ADULT YEARS

All the coaching I did during college as a Rule 10 coach paid off in assisting me in getting my first job. Coaching three sports in the Bonner Springs, Kansas school district meant if they did not have a teaching position for me they would have to find a new coach for all three sports. So my first job was teaching 6th grade science at an intermediate school in the Bonner district and continuing to coach my three sports of volleyball, basketball, and track. That first year had all the normal challenges of a first year teaching but additionally the building was under construction and the crew was literally building a new school around our classrooms. One time the jack hammering was so loud on the other side of my classroom that I was yelling at the top of my lungs our lesson. The jack hammering stop but I kept talking very loudly and one of my students raised his hand and said, "Om, Miss Caldwell, I don't think you have to yell any more, they stopped." Another time we had to leave our classrooms for several days so we gave the Iowa Test of Basic Skills in the gymnasium. Being a building under that much construction meant there were pipes and ductwork and all kinds of things showing in the ceiling. As I was working with a student at my desk brown colored, liquid started pouring from one of the pipes; right onto my desk, all over the papers, student work, my grade-book, and the two of us sitting there. We quickly jumped up and out of the way but we were never quite sure as to what was leaking. Life's Little Lesson – In the middle of challenging circumstances there are probably people there with us.

Our core academic teaching team with one hundred students participated in the local community clean up day. We were assigned to one of the city parks and our responsibilities include picking up trash and tree limbs. The students did an amazing job of working hard to clean up the park. As we were loading the bus to return to school one student asked to use the restroom port-a-potty. Several minutes had passed and I looked in the direction of the restroom and coming from the top vents was a little, gray stream of smoke. Life's Little Lesson – Smoking in the boy's room takes on a whole new meaning when the boy's room is a port-a-potty.

Educational Field Studies (EFS) is an organization that sponsors teacher and student trips to various locations with an emphasis on science education with some cross-curricular connections. I had the opportunity to attend one of the teacher training trips to Orlando, FL in order to learn the various educational components and to determine the fit for connections to our 8th grade science curriculum. Following the trip I determined the program called Ecoquest was the best fit for our curriculum and began discussions with our science department, building administrator, and district personnel as to the process in order to provide this opportunity to our 8th grade students. Given the go ahead from all building and district administrators we presented our idea, cost, and my experience to our group of 8th grade students and their parents. We included connections to the curriculum and I gave background information on the organization as well as the activities students would be involved in. The positive response was overwhelming. In the spring of that school year ten adults took fifty-two 8th grade students on the trip of a lifetime. We rode airboats in the swamp, held alligators and snakes, dissected a shark, snorkeled in the ocean, rode on a boat, hike on an island, saw dolphins swimming in the wild and participated in two educational activities at Epcot Center in Orlando. Beside the hard hallway floor where I slept each night the trip was amazing. It was also the first airplane trip for the majority of our students which provided entertainment of itself. Not always a quiet group at the places we went, I must say they were polite and respectful group and although it was hundreds of miles away from the normal, local field trip this was by far the best! Life's Little Lesson – Give firm expectations, be a great role model and children will live up to the standard.

One school day morning as I and my teaching partner were doing hall duty we had two students bring in a fifty-two ounce jug and excitedly approach us. "Ms. Caldwell, look what we found," they said. One of them gently opened the lid and both my teacher friend and I bent over to peer inside. The entire bottom of the jug and three fourths of the way up the side was covered with intertwining, black, leathery, pipe-shaped skin with two heads moving around. As I was replacing the lid my teaching partner let out the loudest scream that people from all over the building came to our hall to see what was going on. The jug contained two snakes which the students had caught. We put the garter snakes in an aquarium in my science classroom and fed them two goldfish. All of the students enjoyed watching the snakes eat so every class throughout the day asked if we could feed them. Life's Little Lesson – You never know what will show up in your classroom on any given day.

During one summer I took some additional time off in July from teaching swimming lessons and traveled with Lyle, Jan, and Marc to Oregon. We met a group of travelers ready to ride their bicycles along the coast on Highway 101. Famous for its hilly climbs, steep descents and picturesque views it was a bicycle enthusiast dream come true. While Lyle and the other cyclists made their way along the highway by bike, Jan, Marc, and I would sight see. We visited every lighthouse along the Oregon coast, stopped in quaint little towns to shop, purchased salt water taffy at every shop we watched them making it, played at several beaches, and even went whale watching one day. There were camping locations organized along the trip route, one of the coolest was where, just on the other side of a hill, was the ocean. We went to sleep with the sound of lapping water and gentle waves and woke to the sound of bunches of sea lions barking orders to each other. It was by far the most beautiful trip I have ever experienced. Life's Little Lesson – There is no such thing as having to much salt water taffy but there is a problem with that many wrappers in the car.

I had the opportunity to mentor and tutor one of my middle school students through his eighth and ninth grade years. During these two years of during the day contact and after school time his English increased and he made steady progress in his homework completion, grades, and behavior. See this student had decided since he struggled with academics mostly from a language barrier he would become the class clown and he was talented! His disruptions could take an important educational moment and turn it into a stand-up comedy act with the entire class off track and laughing. Having him in class and then seeing him after school gave me the chance to discuss many of these disruptions so that moving into ninth grade they were less disruptive and more at appropriate times. He got suspended during his ninth grade year for fighting and we had a serious conversation about the events. When I asked him what he could have done instead of punching the guy. Thinking I would get an answer like I could have walk away, I could have told an adult… this was his response, "Well, I guess I could have verbally assaulted him." Not exactly where I was headed with the question. Life's Little Lesson – Ask enough questions and you will always get an answer that surprises you.

While teaching 8th grade science at a local middle school our team of core teachers decided to take our students to the state capital and the Natural History Museum located near the capital. The day was well planned and we had a good number of parent volunteers providing extra watchful eyes as we ventured out with one hundred plus students. At the state capital my group was thoroughly entertained by a volunteer docent who toured us through the large, brightly decorated rooms with historical meaning at every turn. This man managed to capture the attention of all 8th graders and adults in his group through the use of stories, songs, and connections which linked Kansas historical events to our learning and memory. He was intelligent, funny, and entertaining. Best trip to the capital I had ever experienced. Following a break for lunch my group eagerly approached the museum for what we hoped would be an afternoon of connections, songs, and entertaining stories designed to stretch our understanding of Kansas and History in general. Our hopes were dashed when our museum docent began by reading the pamphlet of information for the museum highlights. Needless to say our morning docent was a shining star compared with this "Ferris Bueller" type teacher/docent in the pm. Once on the trek through the museum our interest picked up as we were surrounded by historical artifacts and displays of all types. Many of which were direct links to topics covered in the 8th grade History/ Social Science curriculum. However, our boredom with the docent increased through every turn as he enlightened us by reading from the displays in a monotone, dry voice. I noticed several boys having a conversation near the wooly mammoth tooth display. As I moved in closer I could hear them discussing the size of the tooth and then one of them said, "Ross you would be a snack to him (him referring to the wooly mammoth)." Ross who happened to be on the shorter side of his 8th grade growth spurt was rather shorter than most of his classmates and the boys all giggled. I leaned in and without considering the consequences said "he would be more like a tic tac" and we all lost control. Laughing uncontrollably I and the two boys had to remove ourselves from the tour in order to restore our composer. Life's Little Lesson - Just because you think it, it doesn't always have to be said.

After teaching in the classroom for nine years I decided to pursue a job as an instructional coach and new teacher mentor. The Instructional Resource Teacher (IRT) job with my local school district provided such an opportunity. I applied, interviewed, and was offered the position. What a privilege it was to join that group of teacher leaders and work closely with those IRTs already working with secondary new teachers. I grew so much during those many years as an IRT educationally, as a leader, and personally. Even as group dynamics changes over the years and people came and went I always had an amazing group of highly qualified, wonderful individuals to work with. Through my time as an IRT I had the opportunity to present educational staff development sessions on numerous topics, provide one-on-one coaching to new and struggling educators, enhance my technology skills as well as participating in staff development to increase my own knowledge and understanding of educational theory and topics. Life's Little Lesson – Not everyone who goes into education is meant to be a teacher.

It was going to be a routine surgery, one which I even debated about being there for and having to use a sick day, planning for a guest teacher, and all the work that goes into being absent from a teaching position. But Mom and Jan (wonderful family friend; Lyle and Jan call me their adopted daughter) were both scheduled for surgery on the same day at two different hospitals. Our lives were changed forever that cold November 2, 2002 day, when about two hours into surgery the surgeon came out and summoned us to a small kids playroom. We sat in these small chairs listening to her say she decided to remove the ovaries and upon making that incision discovered cancer. It was colon cancer which had started on the outside of the colon. A general surgeon had been called in to remove what could be removed and to determine the extent of cancer involvement. Prior to leaving this somber, quiet room she said there was Liver involvement and in a very kind, compassionate voice said how sorry she was for the news. This quiet, playful room quickly turned to a spinning, crashing, loud room as the shock, terror, questions, and unknowns invaded my mind. With inner turmoil we all returned to the waiting area where the shock continued as we faced the endless barrage of questions in our mind and waited for an update from the surgeon. The evening of my Mom's surgery was scheduled a state playoff game for the high school soccer team, for which I was an assistant coach. I had already planned to meet the team at the field but had not prepared ahead for going straight to the field for the game. I stopped on my way and bought several warm clothing, sports items and met the team. I remember that as the cold, November, Kansas wind blew across the field and onto my face I kept thinking I was in a dream and would wake up soon. Many people report a similar feeling when faced with life altering news, such as the news we had received earlier that day but until you have been there and experienced it there is really no way to justly and honestly describe this experience. Suffice to say if you have had this challenge you "get it" if you have not my hope is you will never have to; but more than likely the journey of life at one time or another will bring a similar experience and you can think back to these words and know you are not alone. Life's Little Lesson - There are others with life scars, who've traveled this path, or one very similar, and they "get it."

My Brother and I took my Mom to her Oncologist appointment and first Chemotherapy treatment. We saw the doctor first and as I feared the news was not good. Progression of the disease and involvement of the Liver put this as a stage four colon cancer. His prognosis was not very encouraging but we were praying to the ultimate healer. The fight was lined out and appointments were set, we went to lunch prior to the scheduled chemotherapy time and at lunch my Mom tried to encourage us. She told us how blessed she has been, what wonderful children she has, and about all the amazing things she has been able to do. She said she was going to fight this but that it was all in God's hands. Her faith seemed unshaken and she knew that no matter the outcome good or bad, life or death, things would work out through God's sovereignty. Life's Little Lesson - God is in control and will take care of you if you have given your heart and life to Him.

The following Eulogy is what I share at my Mom's funeral. I wrote and spoke about several important life lessons my Mom taught me.

My cubicle at the Instructional Resource Center has seen many visitors this year. On one visit a district employee wanted to check in and see how my Mom was doing, as was the case with many of those who stopped by my desk. Following my standard response of she's hanging in there... this person said, "You know your Mom could teach a rock to read." I shared this story with my Mom and for the remainder of her time this school year working with kids she would refer to them as her little pebbles when telling us stories and successes from her day. Throughout my Mom's career she has taught many lessons to many "pebbles" as she called them. As her daughter, I have often been on the learning end of some of the greatest life lessons she has taught. I would like to share a few of the lessons I have learned with you today.

Many of you know I was quite passionate about playing soccer as I was growing up. While my parents were proud of my athletic accomplishments and me it was never a passion for them. They often motivated me to clean my room or follow some direction by threatening to take away a soccer game or practice. However, having never been coached, critiques, yelled at, or judges by my parents on my playing ability, it was my Mother who had the biggest impact on my athletic endeavors. It was on the ride home from a game when my Mom turned around in the car and stared me down with those deep, dark brown eyes and said if you get scored on as the goalkeeper and you lay on the ground upset and disappointed like the goalie from the other team you just played today, I will come out there on the field and pick you up and pull you out of the game. From that time on, even through high school varsity soccer when I failed to save the ball and the other team scored, I could hear my Mom saying get up, don't lay there... the game is not over, if you tried your best that's what matters. I guess that philosophy applies to much more in life than just on the athletic field.

The second lesson brings me to my senior year of high school. What a year! This was a very stressful time in my life and making a college decision was a difficult task for me to accomplish. My Mom gave me this verse from Psalms 84 in the bible, "For the Lord God is a sun and a shield, the Lord bestows favor and honor; no good thing does he withhold from those whose walk is blameless." I have found myself reviewing this promise from God often this past year and praising God for allowing me to grow up being loved and nurtured by godly parents and a Mother whose teaching included the Word of God.

For the final lesson I will share with you today, you may be thinking it would be something about the courage my Mom displayed during her fight with cancer or how her faith and hope in a loving, saving God remained strong through the struggle and while all of those things are very true and very important about my Mother this is what she has done for me... My and Mom and I love to shop. We mostly like to shop for Kayla and McKenzie, so as should be the case our last shopping trip together was none other than a quick evening trip over to Toys R Us to pick up a few items for Kayla's birthday and Christmas presents for both girls. Fighting through the pain and nausea we went from aisle to aisle looking for just the right gifts for our special girls. Books and educational toys were top priority for Mom and roller blades, soccer balls, and blocks topped my shopping list. In the car ride home my Mom talked to me about how blessed I am. She named some of things in my life that she thought were blessings from God; my new job as an IRT after only teaching in the district for three years, my beautiful new house, a host of wonderful friends and co-workers, getting to own and run the swim program, and being an aunt. She then told me how proud she was of my accomplishments, my educational endeavors and me as a daughter, sister, and teacher. That day she encouraged me to be faithful in my service to God and to trust God.

My Mom has helped me learn many important lessons but many of you have also impacted my life and the lives of my family members. Firsthand experience these last few days, weeks, and months have taught us about your generosity of your time, resources, and energy. Your willingness to put our needs and my Mom's needs ahead of your own is evident through the thoughtful gift of time. From special trips to see my Mom; bringing flowers, gifts, videos, CDs and food to the hundreds of encouraging cards sent in the mail and through email. All of you in some way have been an encouragement and a bright light in a very dark time. We thank God for you and ask Him to richly bless your lives for the support you have sent our way.

In closing, one of my favorite professional athletes, Michael Jordan, said this after his father's passing, "I was lucky to get to have my Dad for 32 years of my life." I too feel blessed to have had my Mom for 32 years of my life.

Life after my Mom went to be with Jesus has never been the same. I used to wonder if anything would ever feel "normal" again. My Dad and I love to go to the movies together. We often would see the action-packed, adventure, shoot'em up type of film like Die Hard, James Bond, Star Trek, or Indiana Jones but for some reason on one of our weekly trips to the movies we picked one called The Family Stone. Neither one of us really knew what is was about and we were about four weeks out past my Mom's death. The movie had been out for a while and we were a small group in the theatre. My Dad and I picked the back of the theatre and the movie began. Let's just summarize this part to say that the mother in the film has cancer and is dying. I know that for three fourths of the film I was sobbing. There were some very funny parts just like real life but the story hit close to my heart and my heart was still hurting so badly. My Dad and I had a conversation in the car that evening about how life goes on around us, people get back to their normal activities but nothing feels like it will ever feel right again. Life's Little Lesson – Life does go on after the death of a loved one and the path is different for each person but eventually you do get to a new "normal."

The T.V. show Survivor is a good analogy for earning a doctoral degree. The goals of the show Survivor are outwit, outlast, outplay in order to be the last one standing but then all those who you outwitted, outplayed, and outlasted have the final say in who gets the million dollars. Similarly when earning a doctoral degree you must outwit (continually fight for your research and coursework) outplay (jump through hoop after hoop after hoop) and finally outlast (preserve through the many revisions) then the committee still is the one to make the decision. Life's Little Lesson – Pick your battles wisely.

I have a Jack Russell Terrier dog named Tucker. He is your typical Jack Russell very busy getting into trouble but very protective of me and his house, he is eager to greet guests, can jump higher than any dog I have seen jump, and can learn to live by a schedule. He knows he is man of the house and is willing to defend his territory if necessary. We learned this the hard way in three different lessons. The first came when my Sister brought their Rat Terrier, Tiger, over to play with Tucker. There was no playing only chasing and fighting. We put them in separate rooms but they continued to growl and bark so much that Jessica finally just took Tiger home. So they are the cousins in the family who do not get along and are separated at all costs. The second time was when Jessica, the kids, and I walked in with a Labrador puppy. We sat the girl puppy on the deck and called Tucker to come visit. He raced up the steps and took one look at her, grabbed her by the neck, started swinging her around and poop was flying everywhere.

The final time was with a 100lb English Bulldog to Tucker's 16lbs. Gordo's (dog's name) head was the size of a bowling ball and he could have taken care of Tucker in one swing of his head but would you believe my dog bullied this 100lb bowling ball head bulldog. Tucker would make this low growl and follow the dog around everywhere. If Gordo sat down Tucker would nudge up against him and make him move. Life's Little Lesson – Take after Tucker's example and protect the people you love.

Chapter 7
Niece and Nephew Time

My Brother and Sister both have children. David and Sarah have Ella (10) and Henry (6) and Jessica and Mitch have Kayla (18) McKenzie (15) and Cooper (11). Having had no children of my own I adore and spoil my nieces and nephews. I enjoy spending time and talking with them. Life's Little Lesson – kids are funny. The following are some of the funny things I have heard or experienced from my nieces and nephews.

- Ella is the quiet but smart one. When she was younger we played the White Elephant gift exchange game but we wrapped all kinds of candy. So we explained the rules, gave an example and proceeded to hand out the numbers randomly. Ella picked the #1 so she choose a gift, unwrapped it and was so excited she found the M&Ms box. Cooper was next so we reviewed the rules for the game and he proceeded to take Ella's box of M&Ms….you are probably about the see this picture unfold as Ella became very emotional and attached to the box of M&Ms. No way was she going to give up her present.
- Henry has become a NASCAR fan! He can tell you the driver of each car and who sponsors the driver. He'll watch the race with my Brother and he knows who is in what place, how many laps they go, and what different drivers are doing. It is amazing, all why he is playing with his own set of cars.
- While my Sister-in-Law was driving Ella to school, they heard a blurb on the radio about a nonprofit that gives horseback riding lessons to kids "having a hard time." Ella listened intently, but didn't quite get it ...Ella said :"Mom, maybe somebody will give money so I can have a horse." Sarah responded, "Well, it's really for kids having a hard time." (I didn't want to explain any further.) Ella then added, "Well, I'm having a hard time!" Sarah then asked "You are? How so?" Ella finished with "I'm having a hard time getting a horse!"
- Sarah shared this… Henry turns 6 today!! This boy loves racing,

NASCAR and anything to do with numbers. One night quite a while back he asked me to "fix the flap on my fenders." He meant that I needed to adjust his nighttime pull-up. He didn't understand why I would be confused...) A couple of nights ago (he's been a little worried about being away from me during Kindergarten) he told me, "The road of life is full of potholes," which he got from a Berenstain Bear book he says, but it really stuck with him.....just his kind of analogy. Can't believe he's 6 and he's been true to form since the day he arrived-a race down the highway at rush hour to the hospital and he made his appearance 30 minutes later. I should have known this guy would be all about speed.

- Kayla and I were driving and we saw a kid dressed in his Halloween costume and I said that goes to show that Halloween is just around the corner. There was a pause and then Kayla said well, that doesn't mean just around the corner, which means it is coming up. I asked her how she got so smart she said she was in kindergarten, so she was smart.
- Kenzie went through a period of time when the doctors thought she had Type 1 diabetes and Jessica was checking her glucose number when she gently used the needle contraption but didn't go deep enough to get any blood so Kenzie quickly volunteered another finger and as honest as could be said that other finger must be empty.
- When Kayla was a toddler she had gone to her room to get some toys to play with and Jessica had not seen her return so she put down the laundry and when she opened Kayla's door there was a cloud of white dust and then she saw Kayla jump on the bed squeeze the baby powder container and land with a poof of white clouds all around and over her.
- Cooper just the other day gave Papa Caldwell (my Dad) a big hug and told Papa he loved him then proceeded to walk out the garage door with his mother and said to her, "I love that guy."
- We have a sub sandwich shop near our neighborhood and their slogan is Freaky Fast Delivery. The shop's name Jimmy John's. Kayla and I were driving and she saw the delivery car and said there goes some Jonny Joe sandwiches instead of Jimmy John's.
- One of the neighbors down the street had a beautiful great dane named oreo. Kenzie started talking about the dog but called it cookie and we were trying and trying to figure out what dog she was talking about and finally it dawned on us, "Oreo" aka. Cookie.
- One morning Cooper enter his Mom's (my Sister's) room while she was still in bed and said, "Mom, Mom, Hey Mom, I need a little help here." My Sister turned over to find him dressed in his three piece pinstripe, navy blue suit with dress shoes on trying to

button the vest over top of the jacket. When she inquired as to why he was so dressed up he said, "I wanted to look handsome today, don't I look handsome?" My Sister helped straighten his suit out and then he went downstairs to show his sisters and they all took pictures of him outside.

- The Suite (sweet) Life of Kayla and Kenzie – after a house fire my Sister's family spent a period of several weeks in a hotel suite while they were looking for a rental house to live in during the reconstruction phase of their own property. The girls got very comfortable with the extended continental breakfast, the swimming pool, and a queen size bed. During this time I replaced the carpet on the stairs in my house and upgraded to a newer, pattern type actual stair carpet with a tight weave for increased durability. It was a dark brown with a light brown color pattern running through it. The first time Kenzie walked in to my house she stop right in her tracks and said, "Whoa, hotel stairs." That's when we knew they had been in the hotel suite a little to long.

- When Kayla was about four years old she went to a special work day with me where teachers were going to be organizing instructional materials for upcoming extended learning opportunities they were going to offer to students in order to increase math and reading skills. I was helping to lead the organization of the reading materials and my co-worker Angel was going to assist with the math materials. During the introduction and overview I made the comment that Angel would be coming in a few minutes to help with the morning activities. When I finished the directions and everyone started working Kayla came over and asked me "How Angel was going to get here." Not yet thinking in a four year old church going brain I asked, "What do you mean?" She replied with, "Is she going to fly here?" We quickly had a deep theological discussion regarding people using bible names or biblical references as ways to name their children. I then said Angel was driving a car and she said okay and went back to her coloring.

- A similar story happened with Kenzie several years later. Angel was coming to my house to drop some dinner off and we had explained to everyone we were going to have a dinner which Angel was bringing. When the doorbell rang Kenzie stood up and flew around the stairway and as she came around she asked, "Is Jesus Here?" When she recognized Angel she seemed disappointed but went and sat down at the table for dinner.

- Something one day was said about Cooper being a Daddy's baby and Kenzie quickly said she was a Mommy's baby and when we got to Kayla, she said she was an Auntie's baby. I love that girl.

My Sister and I are best of friends and I am blessed to live very close to them so I have almost daily contact with her and the kids. Stories from kids could be a book by itself but I have recorded some of the best ones I can remember. To my nieces and nephews both immediate and extended family may I encourage you to keep the joy from God knowing you are loved with a love that died on the cross for you. Knowing your family is so proud of you and the unique place you have in our family. Do the right things right and BE GREAT! Should you fall short of great…pick yourself up, get back on the journey, and try again…we all fail and fall sometimes. Know I love you with a love that cannot even be expressed although in this book I have tried.

Chapter 8
Swim Program Years

My summer job has always been teaching swimming lessons. I have been fortunate to work for the same program for a little over 20 years. It is the program which my Sister and I now own and operate. When I began as a teacher I worked with children of all ages helping them learn to swim. My favorite age group were the three and four year olds because of the funny things they would say and when one was truly scared of the water it was amazing as they overcame that fear and began picking up skills and enjoying the water. In one particular three and four year old class I was trying to go over names and I came to a boy and asked him what his name was. He said, "Batman." I replied, "No, what's your real name." He again said, "Batman. Flustered I thought to ask him, "What does your Mom call you?" He replied this time with, "Oh! She sometimes calls me Kyle." Life's Little Lesson – If at first you don't succeed, try again, then try a different avenue.

Another time when I was teaching I had a boy on parents day (the last class day parents come into the pool area and watch the lesson) do a flip while jumping in and land with his head on the metal pool gutter. The sound echoed through the pool room and I was about 10 yards from the edge since the kids were to jump in and swim out to me. My eyes were as big as saucers and I raced to the edge to pick up what I knew was going to be cracked open head. I saw the Dad meeting me at the side and as I started helping him get out the Dad started in, "how many times have we told you not to do that." Somewhat to my relief because I did not teach that nor had he done that before in lessons. Life's Little Lesson – Listen to your parents it will save you a few headaches...literally

I taught a goldfish class made up of mostly five and six year olds. One of my students, Alfredo, kept leaning over and falling into the pool. I would be away from the side with another students and Alfredo would lean over and plop right in. I would have to pick up the child I was working with and quickly get to Alfredo as he was underwater looking up at me each time. I called for the aide, my sister, and she sat with him on the side. Each time he would start to lean over she would put her arm out to stop him from falling in. Eventually as she stretched out her arm keeping him on the side of the pool he started giving her arm a kiss every time she stretched it in front of him. Life's Little Lesson – It is nice to show your appreciation for a helping hand or in this case a helping arm.

Our staff went to the lake for a weekend of water fun and relaxation. To add to the fun we blew up a water island equipped with a slide, net lounge area, and cup holders. In addition, we had a water trampoline which Kayla, my niece, called the "jumpoline." My Brother-in-law Mitch also brought the boat for towing people around on the three person tube. Mitch drove the boat near the floats in order to shake us up from the wake he created. On one particular round he steered the boat in close to us and misjudged the distance needed for clearance of the tube and there was a great collision. The three person tube met the water trampoline and there was an enormous explosion of bodies flying into the air. Life's Little Lesson – Sometimes even the strangest of things can have an enormous impact on us.

Another time our swim program staff decided to camp out. We got out to the lake early and set up the tents, got the camp area organized and then went to the lake. While on the boat and floating island it began raining. At first it was a light rain but it quickly picked up intensity. Riding in a moving boat with rain coming down is kind of like being hit all at once and then continually with tiny needles all over. We got off the water and back to camp where everything in the tents were soaked. Quickly, I assessed the situation and decided to take everyone back to my house so we drove the hour back. I ordered pizza on the way and the group decided what games to play or movies to watch. I pulled out pillows and blankets; t-shirts and shorts; chips and popcorn and we had a great campout in my house. Life's Little Lesson – You can make a pretty good smores in the microwave.

As the director of the program from time to time I have the privilege of handling a situation with a concerned and/or frustrated parent. Although we strive to provide the best quality swimming lesson in the area and our instructors have expectations of a certain level of behavior we all fall short of those expectations from time to time. In one particular case a mother returned to the pool following her children's lesson and express deep concern and frustration at a conversation one of the instructors had had during the forty-five minute class period and that this instructor had made fun of several of the high schools in the district which the instructor had not attended. I discussed with the parent the situation, my expectations for my staff, expressed my concern and apologized for the situation and we were able to come to a solution which resolved the mother's concerns. Having a parent concerned about their child on passing a class is one thing but having a parent concern about something we said or the way we joked about something was a situation which needed immediate attention. Although the details would be shared directly with the individual instructor involved as well as the plan of action for the following day, I felt strongly this was an opportunity to remind everyone about the language and the impact their words can have on children. I decided at the next class change I would call all the instructors over for a brief instructional meeting while the lifeguard and pool managers monitored the students sitting on the side. Since this had never been done it made a lasting impact on everyone working that day. For the remainder of the day and into the next day my Sister, Jessica (one of the pool managers), had instructors coming up to her and confessing things they had said which were not the best of examples to their students. Life's Little Lesson – Occasionally, we all need reminders about living up to our expectations and being a role model.

I happen to be at the pool one day when one of the smaller kids, he was maybe five years old, immediately stood up turned and looked at my direction. He had a pale, whitish, green look to his face and as the hands went for the stomach I realized what was happening and jumped into action. I scooped the kid up into my arms, with one hand under his chest and the other holding his shorts and I ran toward the trash can. I will forego the details at this point, suffice to say we made it to the trash can in time. Life's Little Lesson – There are certain signs and signals to look for when caring for or teaching children.

Chapter 9
Illness Years

I had just finished presenting my favorite topic, brain research and classroom connections, for teacher staff development in our evening inservice program called Advanced Teaching and Learning. These evening sessions provided district teachers opportunities to learn new strategies for the classroom and to earn professional development points for relicensure or coursework hours toward a master's degree. As I began cleaning up the tables and packing my materials I noticed it felt very difficult to catch my breath. I felt as though I had run a race. A somewhat strange sensation as lung and breathing difficulties had never been a problem for me so I dismissed it as I was overly tired, had a cold earlier in the month, and I was leaving for a conference in the morning. The feeling of shortness of breath or as though I had run a race and was out of breath continued to linger the next day as I traveled with a fellow district employee to Minnesota for the conference. We were both totally pumped and excited about this conference and I knew I did not want anything, especially a health issue, to damper what was going to be an amazing, learning opportunity. Life's Little Lesson – When you stop and think there is something wrong…There probably is.

Well, that was the beginning of a journey with my own mystery diagnosis and medical expedition. Needless to say the educational conference was miserable because of the illness not because of the content or presenters. Those were top-notch as always by the Boomerang Project group. However, about half way through the first full day I was coughing, short of breath, having stomach issues, and pretty much hurt all over. When I couldn't really eat or walk up the steps to our floor at the hotel I knew something was wrong. We had no car so I went to the front desk and asked the desk attendant if there was a walk-in health clinic nearby. I went to a minute clinic and as I started to express some of my concerns I was told I needed to go to a different place for my symptoms. Just down the road from our hotel was a new facility which included both a walk-in health clinic and an emergency room. I was quickly upgraded from walk in to ER patient. I was given IV fluids, anti-nausea medication, and had a battery of medical tests. One of which was a chest x-ray. After viewing the film electronically the doctor came in and said I had pneumonia. He prescribed antibiotics and I was on my way. Somewhere in the back of my head was a little voice saying this does not seem right but I got the antibiotics and headed back to the conference with a pneumonia diagnosis. Life's Little Lesson – if you are waiting in a multiple hour line at the walk in health clinic and you wonder if you need an ambulance it is time to go to the emergency department at the hospital.

A follow up x-ray at my doctor in Olathe confirmed the pneumonia diagnosis and I was prescribed a stronger antibiotic as well as told to take the week off from work. Sunday evening came with little change in my health. Having always recovered quickly after an illness the lingering fatigue and shortness of breath were worrisome. However, I geared up for a day back at work. At noon I decided to call the doctor back and head home because of fatigue, shortness of breath, cough, and chest pain when I took a deep breath. This time in the doctor's office I received two shots, one in each hip of antibiotics and a steroid booster. Besides really painful hips the shots did not help the health situation. Following doctor's orders I remained at home resting another week and also begin using breathing treatments. By Sunday evening I was expecting to feel much better and ready to tackle a busy week back at work, However, I still felt horrible. I went to Lyle and Jan's house for the evening that Sunday evening and ended up crawling into my bed in my room at their house that evening after crying and trying to explain how horribly I still felt even after all this time off and all the medications. Having a follow up appointment scheduled already for Monday, Lyle volunteered to go with me and advocate for getting a specialist involved. The visit with my primary care doctor at that time was short and the following day, on Tuesday, I was sitting in the office of the pulmonologist (Dr. Bradley) who would become invaluable in this health- crisis journey. A pulmonary function test (PFT), an ambulatory O2 test, and a CT scan all confirmed that there was a disease process going on other than pneumonia. The CT revealed a process of inflammation called ground-glass infiltrate which has a glassy, white color look throughout the lungs. My moment of relief about not being crazy quickly faded to a moment of fear, if it is not pneumonia…what is it? What does this mean? How could this happen? After processing time, Dr. Bradley continued with the… what's next phase. Everyone insisted this would be something to diagnose and treat. A week later I found myself checking into day surgery for a bronchoscopy with biopsy. Following that procedure the all clear was given to start prednisone to try to reduce the inflammation in my lungs.

Life's Little Lesson – When you feel beat up, exhausted, and fed up with the medical field find someone who will go and fight with and for you.

With the steroid treatment completed and Spring Break over I returned to work for half days. By Friday I noticed a cramp-like pain in my lower leg that would not go away. Saturday brought an even more intense pain and after talking with the on-call pulmonologist I was headed to the emergency department. That all ended with a five day stay in the hospital for a lower leg deep vein thrombosis (blood clot). Life's Little Lesson – Just when you think there can't be something else…there is.

Meanwhile, the steroids had done nothing to improve my lung function, which was in fact continuing to decrease, and was at forty-seven percent. It was time to try to figure this thing out which meant an open lung biopsy. Doing what is called a video assisted thoracotomy, the heart and lung surgeon collected two different wedges of lung tissue. The lung tissue was studied by the Olathe Medical Center pathologist and then set on for further study by lung pathologist at Mayo Clinic. While waiting for the results I was starting the road to recovery from major chest surgery. Life's Little Lesson – A chest epidural is a wonderful thing.

Drum roll Please… Results were in…Non-Specific Interstitial Pneumonitis most likely with a connective tissue disorder. In other words, we don't really know what is going on in the lungs therefore it is probably linked to an autoimmune disease. The one definite answer from the biopsy was the presence of inflammation. After a battery of blood tests I was referred to a Rheumatologist who diagnosed the autoimmune disease as Sjogren's Syndrome. Somewhat uncommon as a primary diagnosis, Sjogren's most often is a secondary disease which causes dry eyes and dry mouth, however, in my case the immune system has attacked my lungs causing the inflammation and decreased lung function. The goal of treatment became trying to reduce the inflammation and increase lung function. I started taking a daily, oral chemotherapy drug called Imuran in order to tackle the inflammation. Those beginning days were very tough with nausea and fatigue but a few positive, little increases started showing up in my pulmonary function test but quickly leveled off at sixty percent plus or minus several percent on any given day. Life's Little Lesson – Taking after the medical field if you are unsure of something you can use the term Non-Specific as a descriptor such as we are having nonspecific chicken casserole for dinner tonight.

I am harping on the medical field a little in the previous life's little lesson but honestly I have four of the best doctors on my medical team and have been truly blessed by the interest they have taken in my case and the superior care they provide. Once I started the Imuran there seemed to be a constant list of small and annoying complaints. I also started the school year in my Instructional Resource Teacher job with the school district who had worked closely with me and my doctors to agree on responsibilities which would accommodate my health challenges. There was a quick decrease in my immune system due to the Imuran and I began catching every illness going around. In addition, I started having major headaches and stomach issues. The stomach issues led to several tests and in January 2012 removal of my gallbladder. The combination of the lung disease, medication side effects, headaches, catching everything going around, and stress/anxiety led to a joint (my doctors, counselor, and me) decision to stop working in April of 2012. Slightly over a year and the lung disease, an autoimmune condition, headaches added to work had become an overwhelming and impossible combination. The spring I stopped working there were about five principal and assistant principal openings each of which I would have pursued as the next step in my career if I had been well. Life's Little Lesson – Our plan and goals are not always God's plan.

The first time I sat in the rheumatologist office and he began talking about a lung transplant was when the seriousness of this disease hit me. We were a ways from that but he felt it was his responsibility to inform me the path this disease usually takes. In addition to that uplifting news he discussed progression of Sjogren's Syndrome and possible symptoms from taking the Imuran. When we left that appointment my head was spinning with the what ifs, questions, and trying to process what I heard. The combination of all became overwhelming and I had a very difficult time coping. After struggling with sleep disturbances, feelings of hopelessness, and extreme fatigue, I sought help from my pulmonologist and primary care doctor. I also started to see a counselor to work through and process the life-changing recent trend of events. The next time I saw the rheumatologist and we discussed my medication list he asked me why I was depressed. I wanted to scream, "Because you told me I would need a lung transplant," but I managed just to get out that I was overwhelmed by everything and needed a little help to balance my system. At first it was difficult to accept the help from both the medication and my counselor because of the guilt and shame I felt for needing the help. In light of the strength and power of our God and the promises from His word to be with us in times of struggle and to give us strength in Him for the journey we face. I felt like a weak Christian, like I was letting people down. Not only was that completely flawed thinking it kept me in a spinning place, a place in which I could not move forward in this journey. Life's Little Lesson – Occasionally we need outside, unbiased, Christian counseling to help us process where we are in the jungle of emotions, actions, and activities to get us where we want to go on the journey of acceptance and to build strength and faith for what lies ahead.

One of the most debilitating and frustrating parts of this illness has been the daily headaches. Having gone from a headache or two a month to almost daily has been quite an adjustment. I never know exactly when it will hit or how bad it will get. It can range from a dull, annoying type ache to a blood-pounding, extremely painful, emergency room going vice. In my early trips to the emergency department at our local hospital we joked about Marlena's room at Olathe Medical Center but having been there almost monthly if not a couple of occasions in a month there is some truth to it. I could be on a first name basis with several of the doctors if it weren't for all of us being doctors; them doctors of medicine and me a doctor of education. Two years into this headache drama I began seeing a pain specialist in dealing with the headaches. We reviewed the medications which I had taken in attempts to control the headaches. A plan was formed which included new medication and occipital nerve block shots. If you take your hand and cup it around the back of your head that is the occipital lobe and the occipital nerve runs perpendicular to your cupped hand on both the right and left sides. The shot consisted of both a numbing medication and a steroid and was extremely painful when being administered. While hoping the shots would provide some relief, the medication I was taking was intended to be preventative in order to avoid getting the headaches in the first place. However, I had a negative reaction to the medication which included a severe emotional response that caused me to be angry, impulsive, and very depressed. I had vivid nightmares of being killed or killing others. During this time I felt I was going crazy until my counselor and primary care doctor figured out it was the medication adding significantly to the anxiety I was already dealing with as a result of the illness diagnosis and the changes which were occurring. When the medication and occipital shots failed to make any positive changes on the headache front, we decided to try botox in treating migraine type headaches. I received thirty-one bee sting type injections throughout my forehead, around my ears, and in the back of the head and neck area. This type injection is supposed to last around three to four months and let's just say these were some of the most uncomfortable and painful months to get through. Prone to what one would call strange reactions, the botox paralyzed some of my neck muscles leaving weaker ones to take on more work causing those muscles to tire quickly and not want to work as well. During part of this time I was helping to coach soccer and on one occasion I looked down to help a boy set his feet and kick the ball and I was unable even to look up to see of his kick made it in the goal. I kept telling my family and friends I had a bowling ball sitting on top of my neck and my muscles were screaming at me to get it off. My pain management doctor, the neurologist I saw after this, and my primary care doctor had never seen such a reaction to the botox. Life's Little Lesson – This was the phase of "if it can go wrong, it will." It was important to have family and friends to support, encourage, and provide reminders of God's sovereignty.

My pulmonologist sent me to National Jewish Health hospital in Denver, Colorado for a consultation and recommendation on a treatment plan. Dr. Bradley (my pulmonologist) confers with the lung specialists at National Jewish often about current research, treatment plans, and unique cases such as mine. I was scheduled for a five day trip which included meeting with the doctors for discussion, answering questions, and exam; a plethora of tests and consultations; then the week concluded with an exit session with the main pulmonologist where he presented the team's conclusions and recommendations. One of the tests I completed was an exercise oxygen level test. I was hooked up to all kinds of machines, masks, and IV's all while on an exercise bike. They could measure the amount of air coming in, how much was being used, how much was exhaled, the level of oxygen in the blood and the rate of respiration. In preparation for this test, one of the nurses had to put in an arterial IV line. Unfortunately the artery in my wrist was not cooperating and the IV would not go in but it made a nice big hole in the artery and blood started spurting everywhere. We got it wrapped and he started to clean up the mess of blood which was literally everywhere in this small room. He said, "I am going to clean up my mess and then we will try again." I responded with, "Technically that is my mess, all over." We both had a good laugh. Second try worked and I was on the bike riding. I had a nice three minutes of riding and then they started the test. Every minute they would increase the difficulty of the bike and as I was working would record the oxygen data. I kept going, I kept working. They would ask me can you go one more minute and I would say yes. I was willing to keep trying minute after minute. Finally, the question came, can you go one more and I hesitated on my response, barely managed to get out let's try but they said that was good. I somehow managed to get unmasked, untangled in the lines of tubing, and made it to the lounge chair. The room was spinning, I felt like throwing up, and I was so out of breath they put oxygen on for me. The bike/exercise test was by far the coolest and newest test I did while at National Jewish. I also completed a pulmonary function test, an echocardiogram for heart function, a six minute walking oxygen level test, I met with a physical and occupational therapist, and had multiple blood tests to round out the testing portion of my time at National Jewish. During the concluding meeting with the main pulmonologist he specifically mentioned the bike test and that they had never seen anyone go so long with such a low level of oxygen. Most people generally have an oxygen saturation level of 99% to 100% even I with lung disease while sitting hover between 95% and 100%. However, during the exercise test my oxygen level dropped to 72% and I was still going on the bike. Life's Little Lesson – You never know exactly how far you can go, how much you can endure, and what you can overcome until the test (situation) is over.

    After meeting with the main pulmonologist at National Jewish Health and hearing similar information about the disease's current stability but depressing prognosis my emotions were wildly out of control. It looked promising that my lung function had leveled off rather than continuing the downward, spiral trend it was on. However, it did not appear that I would regain much additional lung function as it had seemed to stabilize rather than continuing to improve. I was also reminded of the very great possibility that no matter what the medication, the progression of the disease meant that eventually my lung function will decrease and become so impaired that I would need a lung transplant. At any age that is a lot of information to take in but the fact was once again there were no answers and in fact seemed like more questions even. At thirty-eight years old, having just finished a doctorate degree in education having to deal with lung disease and its effects were really not on the agenda. The week had been overwhelming in many aspects. We had been so busy we had no time for tourist activities but now on the last day we were finished with the meetings, had completed all the tests and it was time to wait for our flight back to Kansas. At that moment I really did wish I was Dorthy, from the movie the Wizard of Oz, so I could just click my heels and return home. As my Dad went to get the car I sat with our family friend Lyle and was overwhelmed by the emotions and feelings from the week. I cried and sobbed, my head hurt, my heart was sad, and I felt stuck with no place to run. The news was the same and I had such high hopes of a different outcome. I was at a precipitous in my career with several pathway options including being a building principal or working in district leadership. So many options but now this…lung disease. I had never smoked in my life, never been exposed to chemicals, and hardly even been sick. While my mind was still racing and emotions were flying we decided to take a quick trip into the mountains outside Denver before we needed to be at the airport. I rested in the backseat listening to music and a recording of a relaxation technique, which my counselor Becky had made for me as a podcast, as we made our way up into the steep mountains. We came to a small mountain town that had an outlet shopping area. They had an Under Armour and NIKE store so we went shopping. Life's Little Lesson

– Shopping can soothe the soul, especially when you are purchasing sporty items for the little ones in the family.

I had been working half days but on a full-time contact, however, the district human resources administration started having conversations with me about what the second semester was going to look like since I was out of sick days. We decided on a half time contact which meant I could keep my insurance coverage as normal without any changes but I would be receiving less money each paycheck working only half time. At this time as a single homeowner finances became a huge area of concern in this now almost full year illness journey. As the Spring semester progressed so did the decrease in my immune system and I began catching everything going around. In addition, my emotional well-being was paying a high toll in trying to keep up a somewhat normal schedule under very not-normal physical conditions. Toward the end of March of that second semester a joint decision between myself, Dr. Bradley (my pulmonologist) and Dr. Eliason (my primary care doctor) was made to take an unknown, unspecified amount of time off of work due to the Autoimmune Lung Disease and a host of other complications. After thirty days off of work for an illness or injury I could apply for short term disability and for the follow six months receive a check somewhat similar to my previous paychecks. However, looking to the future in order to apply for social security disability it was a 180 day waiting period of being off work and then you could apply. Once you apply it is still several months before a decision is made and as I was told by numerous people most everyone is denied the first time they apply. This was true in my case. Several months past after filing my claim and then the denial letter came. Life's Little Lesson – It does not matter the circumstances any denial letter addressed to you is devastating.

As the 2012-2013 school year started and I was not working, the months of July, August, and September were terrible months for me. Depression and anxiety ruled my innermost world. I could hardly walk through the school supply section of any store without tears flooding my eyes. Everything and everywhere reminded me of what I should be doing and where I should be doing it. My life was a dark cloud and I was living in and longing for the past. As people would ask me how the school year was going or what I was doing I choked back the lump in my throat and the tears which immediately developed in my eyes and usually responded with I was on medical leave for a lung disease. A very true statement I managed to get out but my heart longed for the normalcy of a daily job, of the interaction with others, of the leadership opportunities, of friendships, and of making a difference in schools. My self-worth was wrapped up in what I did rather than whose I am and what Jesus did for me on the cross.

I struggled for over a year with anxiety and panic attacks. The fear of the future, the fear of not knowing, and the fear of questions would trigger the anxiety which would rumble around creating chaos in my brain then the out of control, spinning feeling began and I would move into a panic attack with feeling like I couldn't breathe, sweaty, lightheaded, and fearful. I felt a tremendous need to run, run away, where to I don't know but the feeling of running away added to the overall stress of the anxiety. I received very helpful tools and knowledge from my counselor Becky and she was available several times in those days by phone and email in addition to our weekly session. For most of this first year I hid much of this depression, anxiety, and panic attacks from my family and even to some extent from Lyle and Jan. In the midst of the worst of the storm my behavior may have screamed I have a problem with depression and anxiety but the words coming from my mouth to the ears of my family took some time and work. Let me clarify that I have plenty of family love and support but in my own anxiety filled, twisted sense of reality I felt like I would be adding to their stress, placing a burden, being a burden, and there were my own feelings of shame, guilt, and unworthiness wrapped up in this spinning web of depression deception. This anxiety cycle began to wear on me and there were times I questioned my trust and faith in God. I questioned my purpose and the worthiness of my life; I for brief moments here and there throughout this process questioned my own ability to keep doing this illness life and in a few of those heart, heavy moments Satan's lies about suicide flooded my mind. Life's Little Lesson – Thank God…You don't have to do this life on your own ability. God is greater and He has a destiny for your life; one of HOPE.

    The epiphany of the previous life's little lesson did not happen overnight and to say it has cured the depression and anxiety would also be false. However, God started a work in my heart which is leading to a change in my head. In the Spring semester of 2013 I began attending a ladies church bible study once a week. We used a Beth Moore study on Fruit of the Spirit and God began working on me, softening my heart, training my spirit, and touching my spinning, out of control mind. Beth Moore's studies have a way of getting you into the Word of God and making it personal no matter the subject. In that first study there were connections and convictions but change started to occur in the second Beth Moore weekly study I began. This was during the Fall semester of 2013. Our ladies bible study group leaders chose the study DAVID, Seeking a Heart Like His. I would say they had me in mind when they choose this study but I know that was not true. Week one, day two kicked things off for God's intervention in my life. The verse is 1 Samuel 15:22 "But Samuel replied: Does the Lord delight in burnt offerings and sacrifices as much as in obeying the voice of the Lord? To obey is better than sacrifice and to heed is better that the fat of rams'"; the study question...What does verse 22 mean to you? My God inspired connection- listening and following or obeying is key; not what we can do, bring or even be. Life's Little Lesson – Seek God, do a bible study, get into His word, read God inspired books; do whatever you can do to hear God speaking to you.

During this journey I have had many procedures, surgeries, tests, and lab work. One of these happened to be an early morning spinal tab at a downtown large hospital. My Sister was going to go with me in order to drive home. Little did I know that one of our best Tres Dias (Tres Dias is a non-denominational religious organization which provides opportunities for spiritual growth and renewal. Also a wonderful adventure to meet new people who will travel the ups and downs with you.) friends Michelle came to surprise me and go with us. Once I was set up and answered the same question three times in a row Michelle and Jessica were allowed back to stay with me until it was my turn to go in. We were making jokes and playing around so much that the two of them got kicked out and had to go back to the family waiting area. I just smile even thinking of that now and how funny things were. Who gets kicked out of the surgery/patient waiting area? Life's Little Lesson - Life is not very fun if you don't ever get kicked out of a waiting room for being funny.

I was still struggling to find any help for the debilitating migraine headaches I experience on a daily basis. After various kinds of medication failed to make a difference I decided to try a rather new procedure where a neuro-stimulator is placed with leads above my left eye and the battery down into my chest. Then the line snakes through my head, behind my ear, into my chest to connect the two together. When I use it I have various settings which sends a signal to the lead for what is supposed to be a soothing stimulation or massage type feeling. I was at home recovering from this surgery when during a family dinner I sneezed and felt an incredibly painful pinch in my forehead and then I kept saying something is falling in my head, above my eye. Turns out the lead popped loose and recoiled back to around my ear and that was the falling feeling. I return to the surgeon's office and immediately was sent for an X-ray. Then it was back to the operating room to redo the complete surgery again. It has not been the answer I was hoping for but it is sometimes good for a massage-type feeling for just above my left eye and temple area. Life's Little Lesson - Sometimes things just break, even if it's been sown into your head.

I wish this closing paragraph ended with a miraculous healing and the lung disease and autoimmune disease were completely gone. I wish I could tell you I am back at work full time touching the lives of students, teachers, and parents. I wish I could say how the change in my spirit effected change physically but I can't. I remain at sixty percent lung function, getting out of breath if I walk to far, up a hill or stand and talk for to long. I remain plagued with almost daily, migraine type headaches associated with the autoimmune disorder. I have applied for disability (which is a book in and of itself) and continue the daily battle with pain and medication side effects. The anxiety and depression are companions but no longer consistently control my thoughts thanks to God, Becky, and my extended family with 10 nieces and nephews who daily amaze me, entertain me, and make me smile. I am going to finish with a final life's little lesson- this one I learned in a song as a child growing up in the church but have been reminded of in these days of spiritual renewal. "I am a promise, I am possibility I am promise with a capital P and a great big bundle of potentiality and I am trying to hear God's word and I am trying to make the right choice and I am a promise to be anything God wants me to be."

Life's Little Lessons Master List

Life's little lesson – If there is an open door…go through it!

Life's little lesson – Be creative in finding solutions to the problems you face.

Life's little lesson – Family plays such an important part in our memories.

Life's Little Lessons – Goodbyes are hard on everyone.

Life's little lesson - This was a painful life lesson for my Brother but we both learned to look up when you are racing down a hallway, you never know what could be sticking out of the wall.

Life's little lesson – The playground can be a tough place even when you are following the examples and rules.

Life's little lesson – Big moments in life should be shared with family.

Life's little lesson – don't run with eggs in your hand.

Life's little lesson – always stick up for family but not necessarily through fighting.

Life's little lesson – when you find something you love and you devote time to learning it well; you never know where it will take you.

Life's little lesson – if you break it…fix it, no matter the cost.

Life's little lesson - The seatbelt law! Obey it.

Life's little lesson – Make goals and then challenge yourself to break them.

Life's little lesson – I enjoyed having an Open "House" Policy.

Life's little lesson – There is treasure all around us, sometimes it is just covered by dirt.

Life's little lesson – There are moments in life which need to be caught on video in order to win $10,000.

Life's little lesson – Parents sometimes do things for their children they would have never tried on their own.

Life's little lesson – Play Hard! No matter what you are doing! Success and fun are bound to be a part, if you are giving all you have!

Life's little lesson – You can make just about anything out of some string, a gum wrapper, and tape.

Life's little lesson - Never, never put important tickets in your mouth.

Life's little lesson – Sometimes just embrace and go for playing in the pouring rain.

Life's little lesson – some decisions are better left to your parents and you just follow their lead.

Life's little lesson - If your gut is telling you something LISTEN to it.

Life's little lesson - When someone in the canoe decides to bail you best decide quickly to jump with them.

Life's little lesson – When you find a best friend nurture the relationship.

Life's Little Lesson – When you make the right decision stick with it no matter what anyone says.

Life's little lesson – Sometimes when the pressure is on you just have to stop and juggle.

Life's little lesson – My Dad is proof that good things can come from Alabama.

Life's little Lesson – seek first knowing and glorifying God.

Life's little lesson – You cannot be worried about what other people think when God is clearly sending you a message. In my case, at this time in my life, soccer was not as important as my emotional and spiritual health.

Life's little lesson – Sometimes prayers are answered with new opportunities which allow us to see gifts and interests we never knew we had.

Life's little lesson – God really can use all circumstances to glorify Him.

Life's little lesson – Sometimes God doesn't just close a door, he slams it.

Life's little lesson - Sometimes it is extremely helpful to be wearing two shirts.

Life's little lesson – Little celebrations are great ways to thank those people who have made a difference in your life.

Life's little lesson – In the middle of challenging circumstances there are probably people there with us.

Life's little lesson – Smoking in the boy's room takes on a whole new meaning when the boy's room is a port-a-potty.

Life's little lesson – Give firm expectations, be a great role model and children will live up to the standard.

Life's little lesson – You never know what will show up in your classroom on any given day.

Life's little lesson – There is no such thing as having too much salt water taffy but there is a problem with that many wrappers in the car.

Life's little lesson – Ask enough questions and you will always get an answer that surprises you.

Life's little lesson - Just because you think it, it doesn't always have to be said.

Life's little lesson – Not everyone who goes into education is meant to be a teacher.

Life's little lesson - There are others with life scars, who've traveled this path, or one very similar, and they "get it."

Life's little lesson - God is in control and will take care of you if you have given your heart and life to Him.

Life's little lesson – Life does go on after the death of a loved one and the path is different for each person but eventually you do get to a new "normal."

Life's little lesson – Pick your battles wisely.

Life's Little Lesson – Take after Tucker's example and protect the people you love.

Life's little lesson – kids are funny

Life's little lesson – If at first you don't succeed, try again, then try a different avenue.

Life's little lesson – Listen to your parents it will save you a few headaches… literally

Life's little lesson – It is nice to show your appreciation for a helping hand or in this case a helping arm.

Life's little lesson – Sometimes even the strangest of things can have an enormous impact on us.

Life's little lesson – You can make a pretty good smores in the microwave.

Life's little lesson – Occasionally, we all need reminders about living up to our expectations and being a role model.

Life's little lesson – There are certain signs and signals to look for when caring for or teaching children.

Life's little lesson – When you stop and think there is something wrong… There probably is.

Life's little lesson – if you are waiting in a multiple hour line at the walk in health clinic and you wonder if you need an ambulance it is time to go to the emergency department at the hospital.

Life's little lesson – When you feel beat up, exhausted, and fed up with the medical field find someone who will go and fight with and for you.

Life's little lesson – Just when you think there can't be something else… there is.

Life's little lesson – A chest epidural is a wonderful thing.

Life's little lesson – Taking after the medical field if you are unsure of something you can use the term Non-Specific as a descriptor such as we are having nonspecific chicken casserole for dinner tonight.

Life's little lesson – Our plan and goals are not always God's plan.

Life's little lesson – Occasionally we need outside, unbiased, Christian counseling to help us process where we are in the jungle of emotions, actions, and activities to get us where we want to go on the journey of acceptance and to build strength and faith for what lies ahead.

Life's little lesson – This was the phase of "if it can go wrong, it will." It was important to have family and friends to support, encourage, and provide reminders of God's sovereignty.

Life's little lesson – You never know exactly how far you can go, how much you can endure, and what you can overcome until the test (situation) is over.

Life's little lesson – Shopping can soothe the soul, especially when you are purchasing sporty items for the little ones in the family.

Life's little lesson – It does not matter the circumstances any denial letter addressed to you is devastating.

Life's little lesson – Thank God...You don't have to do this life on your own ability. God is greater and He has a destiny for your life; one of hope.

Life's little lesson – Seek God, do a bible study, get into His word, read God inspired books; do whatever you can do to hear God speaking to you.

Life's Little Lesson - Life is not very fun if you don't ever get kicked out of a waiting room for being funny.

Life's Little Lesson - Sometimes things just break, even if it's been sown into your head.

I am going to finish with a final life's little lesson- this one I learned in a song as a child growing up in the church but have been reminded of in these days of spiritual renewal. "I am a promise, I am possibility I am promise with a capital P and a great big bundle of potentiality and I am trying to hear God's word and I am trying to make the right choice and I am a promise to be anything God wants me to be."

PART TWO

SONGS, STORIES, SCRIPTURE

I have been blessed since the 9th grade with two sets of parents. My Mom and Dad and also Lyle and Jan. Love, support, encouragement, a safe place to vent and share are just a few of the characteristics of my two sets of parents. All four are amazing educators, great listeners, and wonderful role models. While Jan and I were on a car trip to her mother's house we listened to one of the local Christian radio stations and the song *Long Way Home* by Steven Curtis Chapman came on. Jan said after the song was over that it was the first time in a long time she had heard me sing. I responded with I am living that song right now. We talked about the song and then she wondered what would be the one song/hymn she would pick as her "life" song. This thought struck me and I was on a mission to find the one song that connected my view of the world, my Christian walk, and my life experiences. One song couldn't do it but I came up with a list of twenty-four songs that pretty much cover everything. I also worked on my list to include a variety of artists with varying types of style of music. So this section includes phrases or lines from the song, a story, thoughts, or connections, and a bible verse or verses linking it all together. My hope is you would listen to the song if you have it in your playlist or listen to the free preview on itunes, then read the story and the verse and give yourself time to make your own connections. Somewhat like a daily devotional… each song could be a new day.

Never Let Go – David Crowder Band

When waters rise and hope takes flight oh my soul oh my soul, oh my soul, Ever faithful ever true, you are known, you never let go, When cloud brought rain and disaster came oh my soul, oh my soul, When the waters rose and hope had flown, oh my soul, oh my soul, oh my soul, Ever faithful, ever true, you are known, you never let go.

Imagine being awaken in the middle of the night by a blaring fire alarm. The night's peaceful sleep turns into a panic of commotion as you realize the house really is on fire and everyone needs to immediately get out. This was just the scene during a cold, December night at my Sister and Brother-in-law's house. Flames had engulfed the front door and were moving quickly along the inside wall and through the living room. Jessica (my sister) grabbed my nephew Cooper and headed to the neighbor's house. Mitch (my brother-in-law) ran around to the front to check out the scene and also was in the process of calling 911. Fire engines, an ambulance, and the battalion chief began to show up and spring into action. After sending gallons of water to the front door and entry way the fire fighters thought the fire was under control and limited to just the front entryway and living room. However, fire was burning in the framing and insulation of the upstairs, which eventually burst into flames and filled the bedrooms with black smoke and fire. Water poured down on the house to try to stop the spread of the fire.

The following days included sorting what could be saved from what needed to be trashed in the house, as well as, sorting the amazing amount of donations they received from church groups, community organizations, and each of their workplaces. The tasks and record keeping were daunting but both Jessica and Mitch kept a positive outlook as they gutted the house down to the studs. Appliances, toys, furniture, the melted Christmas tree and clothes had to be trashed because of the fire and smoke damage. Mitch and Jessica picked out a few household items, furniture and garage items for the restoration company to try to restore. Throughout the process and hassle of having a house fire many people commented on my Sister's ability to laugh, enjoy life, and easily process the tragedy of losing treasures, household items, and other material possessions. Jessica and Mitch knew who was holding them and lifting them up in their time of trouble, turmoil, upheaval, and loss. There was plenty of frustration, sadness, and stress but as our verse says they were positive God was with them; helping to guide the restoration process for both the house and their hearts.

> *So do not fear, for I am with you; do not be dismayed, for I am your God. I will strengthen you and help you; I will uphold you with my righteous right hand. Isaiah 41:10*

Worn – Tenth Avenue North

I'm tired, I'm worn, my heart is heavy from the work it takes to keep on breathing, I've made mistakes, I've let my hope fail, my soul feel crushed by the weight of this world, I know that you can give me rest so I cry out with all that I have left.

When I was a little kid I would play hard during the day at whatever sport or activity all of us neighborhood kids created. Often our games meant running and chasing but if we had enough players it was a soccer or football game. My family lived close enough to our elementary school that we could walk there to play as well. We would play for hours like this and I was all in. When it was finally time to go in after the last game of kick the can or bloody mary, I was a stinky, sweaty, dirty mess. It was there in the bathtub or shower when it hit…the fatigue. I was worn out, my muscles were exhausted, and my mind tired, however, my elementary school brain could not make the connection of my exhaustion being a result of a hard day's worth of play versus feeling ill. I would complain about feeling badly but my parents always said, "you are just worn out from your day, go to sleep and you will feel better." They were right of course because the morning would come and I would be up and ready for another day.

Sleep has a wonderful way of restoring our body and strength to tackle the ups and downs of another day. Isn't it also magnificent that we have a God who can restore our resolve and strength of mind. Our verse today is a promise from God that if our hope is in him our strength will be renewed. What a reassuring promise as we face the challenges of life in a broken and fallen world.

> *But those who hope in the Lord will renew their strength. They will soar on wings like eagles; they will run and not grow weary, they will walk and not be faint. Isaiah 40:31*

Lord I Need You – Matt Maher

Teach my song to rise to you, when temptation comes my way, When I cannot stand I'll fall on you, Jesus you're my hope and Stay, Lord I need you oh I need you every hour I need you, My one defense my righteousness oh God how I need you.

Major thoracic lung surgery was not my plan at age thirty-eight, having just completed a doctorate degree in educational leadership. I was planning a future with staff meetings, classroom observation, lunch duty, and PTA meetings as a building administrator. However, surgery and recovery became the plan. The heart and lung thoracic surgeon did a video assisted thoracotomy with lung biopsy. This meant making the first of three incisions and shoving a one and a half inch tube through the intercostal space between two ribs until reaching the right lung. The second incision was used for pushing tools into the lung space to work with the camera and other instruments from the first incision. A wedge-shape section of lung tissue was taken from both the upper and lower lobes of the lung for the biopsy. The third incision finished the procedure as a chest tube was inserted to assist in re-inflating a collapsed lung. Prior to the entire procedure an epidural was inserted in my back to help with pain management while the chest tube was in place for the first twenty-four hours after surgery.

Most everyone, whether you want to admit it or not, are planners. Our fast- paced, over scheduled society almost demands it. From meetings at work, kid's activities, social gatherings, appointments, church or school events our electronic calendars are overloaded and under-powered. We are ourselves can become overloaded and under-powered with the business of life as we have it planned in our calendars but what about the occasional hospital stay, or the pink slip at work, or the natural disaster? What happens when our plans are crushed beneath a more pressing and urgent situation?

One in which we indeed did not plan for, nor did we have the date written in on the calendar. Where is our hope? Where is our help in the unplanned events of life? Best-selling author Max Lucado in his book *You'll Get Through This; hope and help for your turbulent times* writes, "Good Days. Bad days. But God is in all days. He is the Lord of the famine and the feast, and he uses both to accomplish his will." Isn't it a source of strength to remember that God is in the best of days and he is there beside us wrapping his loving, caring arm around us in the midst of our darkest days.

> *Why are you downcast, O my soul? Why so disturbed within me? Put your hope in God, for I will yet praise him, my Savior and my God. Psalm 42:5*

Cornerstone – Hillsong Live

My hope is built on nothing less than Jesus blood and righteousness. But Holy trust in Jesus name, Christ alone cornerstone, weak made strong, In the Savior's love through the storm he is Lord, Lord of all, When darkness seem to hide His face I rest on His unchanging grace, In every high stormy gale my anchor holds within the veil, Christ alone cornerstone through the storm he is Lord, Lord of all.

Both my nieces enjoy playing basketball. Each of them began playing when they were in Kindergarten. Kenzie, as a third grader, is a scrappy, go getter, all out kind of player, where Kayla, a sixth grader, is a thoughtful, talented, hard-working kind of player. Both of them contribute well on the offensive end by making several baskets but it is their defense which always stands out. Heads up defense and thoughtful playing allowed Kayla to step into the passing lane and steal the other team's pass. She took off on a fast break and looked down the court for a teammate running toward the basket. In a full sprint toward the basket she decided to stop. Using a basketball technique called a jump stop she firmly planted both feet following a slight jump in the air. Not thinking about the amount of momentum she had built up in the sprint toward the basket, Kayla quickly realized she was falling forward. In an effort to save the ball she heaved it in the direction of the closest teammate and proceeded to fall, just barely catching herself before sprawling out on the gym floor.

Hope has momentum! Just as Kayla had picked up momentum sprinting down the court. The more we hope in Jesus Christ the more momentum we have to help carry us through the tough times.

May our Lord Jesus Christ himself and God our Father, who loves us and by his grace gave us eternal encouragement and good hope. 2 Thessalonians 2:16

Long Way Home – Steven Curtis Chapman

> *I set out on a great adventure the day my Father started leading me home, He said there are going to be some mountains to climb and valleys to go through, but I had no way of knowing just hard this journey could be cause the valleys are deeper and the mountains are steeper than I ever would have dreamed... But I know we're going to make it.*

My oldest niece Kayla just finished her first semester in middle school. Every morning when I drop her off for school we tell each other "love you" and I add "be a leader today." We have never really talked about what it means to be a leader, what the characteristics are of a leader. But somehow by the examples of her family, wonderful elementary teachers, and church leaders this girl has a really good understanding of leadership. She is hard-working, seeks to understand, stands her ground on things she believes, and is compassionate. We were about eight weeks into this routine when I said "be a leader" and she giggled and said, "You always say that." As a former middle school teacher I know success in middle school has its foundation on the characteristics of positive leadership.

Although each one of us can point to someone or maybe even several people in our lives which we can say have been true positive examples of leadership, Jesus Christ is the ultimate example of positive leadership.

> *Therefore, since we are surrounded by such a great cloud of witnesses, let us throw off everything that hinders and the sin that so easily entangles, and let us run with perseverance the race marked out for us. Hebrews 12:1*

STRONG ENOUGH – MATTHEW WEST

You must, you must think I'm strong enough to give me what I am going through, Forgive me, forgive me if I'm wrong this look like more than I can do on my own, I know I'm not strong enough to be everything I'm supposed to be, I give up, I'm not strong enough, Hands of mercy won't you cover me, Lord right now I'm asking you to be strong enough, strong enough for both of us.

My oldest niece Kayla asked us a question at dinner one evening which her class had discussed earlier in the school day. She asked, "Would you rather swim across a river with alligators or live on an island with man-eating tigers?" Without hesitation Kayla's eight year old sister Kenzie answered I know which one I would pick. After her pause and all of us prompting her she answered, "I would live on the island with man-eating tigers because I am a woman." As you can imagine laughter erupted at the wit but also the innocence of an eight year old.

Maybe you find yourself looking at a situation with two choices similar to the ones Kayla gave us. You are figuratively facing alligators or tigers and neither option is to reassuring. In fact, if you get right down to the truth of the matter both options are quite scary. Possibly you are dealing with a health concern like myself or maybe financial issues, job questions, or relationship problems. Whatever the concern the fear is real. The anxiety produced by the fear can be overwhelming and overwhelming leads to a cycle of repetition fear, anxiety, overwhelmed.

The cycle can be stopped. The alligators and tigers can be calmed and a deeper peace than our current circumstances can be found. The fear can become truth, the anxiety can become motivation and overwhelmed can become peace. It is not an easy cycle to break and in all honesty there are times it makes itself known again but there is a greater and deeper purpose to hold on to and it is in the song lyrics and verse for today.

> *Trust in the Lord with all your heart and lean not on your own understanding; in all your ways submit to him and he will make your paths straight. Proverbs 3: 5-6*

Even If – Kutless

Sometimes all we have to hold on to what we know is true of who you are, when the heartache hits like a hurricane that can never change who you are and we trust in who you are even if the healing doesn't come and life falls apart and dreams are still undone, you are God you are Good, forever faithful one, even if the healing, even if the healing doesn't come.

Heartache, heartbroken, mind-numbing there are a multitude of words we use in our culture to describe the emotional state one might experience when the healing doesn't come to a loved one. When we are left standing at the bedside wondering how life will proceed without the one we love, without their laugh, their wisdom, and their love. As true as those words are they really do not do justice to the incredible pain and life changing event of losing someone close to you.

I vividly recall the final hours of my Mom's life with inconsistent, labored breathing and lack of response to stimuli. It was six months after her death, during a first aid class review where the video of a person in need of help, gasping for air, sent my mind directly back to her bedside that final night. My whole being was stunned by a moment and the emotions from the past. Thankfully we do not have to live in a stuck place of heartache for it is written in our verse for today nothing can separate us from the love of God… we are more than conquerors when we place our trust in a God who has an ultimate plan.

> *No, in all these things we are more than conquerors through him who loved us. For I am convinced that neither death nor life, neither angels nor demons, neither the present nor the future, nor any powers, neither height nor depth, nor anything else in all creation, will be able to separate us from the love of God that is in Christ Jesus our Lord. Romans 8: 37-39*

Busted Heart – For King and Country

I've got it all figured out, I don't have any doubts, I've got a busted heart I need you now yeah I need you now, hold on to me, hold on to me, don't let me lose my way, hold onto me

During the Spring semester of my freshman year in high school I had a friend killed in a car accident. We played soccer for our high school soccer team and always ran the mile and a half to our practice field together. Although we played on separate teams we bonded on our runs together. The day after the car accident which also took the lives of two other classmates and injured a fourth was eerie to say the least. There was an odd silence throughout the school that lasted all day. Kids processing a life changing event…the death of other kids their own age. Whether you knew them as best friends, acquaintances, or merely passed them in the hall it was a lasting impression of a life changing day. That same day at soccer practice we set out for our daily run to the practice field. Arriving near the end of the pack, coach pulled me aside and asked me how I was doing. Tears, I didn't even know were there, started flowing and my grief from the events of the previous twenty-four hours caught up with me.

It took running to practice without my friend for me to realize I grieved her loss and to work through the concept of her death. Maybe for some of us we avoid the process of grief by avoiding a place or possibly there are deep hurts, loss dreams, or emotional turmoil which we keep hidden in the depths of our heart and we refuse to go there. We refuse to confront it and deal with it. Can you imagine with me the freedom and the release we all would feel if we just turned the grief, the hurt, the loss of dreams and the stress over to God. We took one more, full look as it left on its journey to God.

This is the confidence we have in approaching God: That if we ask according to His will, He hears us. I John 5:14

I Bless Your Name – Selah

Some midnight hour if you should find, you're in a prison in your mind, reach out and praise Him for those chains and they will fall in Jesus name, I bless your name, I bless your name, I give honor give you praise, you are the life the truth the way, I bless your name, I bless your name.

During the past two and a half years I have spent many a midnight hour in a prison in my mind. Having been diagnosed with the lung disease, Non-Specific Interstitial Pneumonitis and Sjogrens (pronounced show-grins) Syndrome, an autoimmune disease, life was drastically changing. In just under three month I had gone from a hard-working, over-committed, gifted educator to a sick, can't catch my breath, anxious individual. The anxiety reared its ugly head in those moments during the night when peaceful sleep had been traded for nightmares and insomnia. Questions flooded my mind as I wondered what life would be like with this disease. I questioned the future, my dreams, my goals. I asked God about his hand in this situation, I pondered what would happen if the lung disease progressed and what it would be like if I needed a lung transplant. The whirlwind of queries and fears included the anxiety of not working which led to an entirely new set of questions about being able to pay my mortgage, pay bills, and live on my own. With the anxiety, panic attacks, and frustration at its worst there were moments of doubts about being able to do this. As terrible migraine headaches and other surgical pain became a part of the scenario the fear of not being able to handle this situation became overwhelming. Anxiety and depression ruled my world day and night.

Thankfully, I have a wonderful family, numerous, supportive friends, and a Christian counselor who help me fight the overwhelming times of anxiety, fear, panic, doubt, and guilt. I can't always praise God for the situation I am faced with but I can praise Him for the people who intervene on His behalf to support me. I can praise Him for Psalm 41 verse 13 as His word is everlasting. I can praise God for who he is ... TRUSTWORTHY!

> *Praise be to the Lord, the God of Israel, from everlasting to everlasting. Amen and Amen. Psalm 41:13*

IN CHRIST ALONE – KEITH AND KRISTYN GETTY

In Christ alone my hope is found, He is my life my strength my song, this cornerstone, this solid ground firm through the fiercest drought and storm, what heights of love what depths of peace When fears are still and striving cease my comforter my all in all, here in the love of Christ I stand.

It was one of the warmer beginning of Fall days in Kansas and after school it felt fairly hot out. My Dad (Papa) walked home with Kenzie and Cooper from school. They were so hot that they talked Papa into letting them play in the sprinkler. While playing in the backyard they moved the sprinkler over just enough that they could swing and still get wet. Only problem with this brilliant idea was the ground under the swings was already dust and dirt and adding water to the mix created a muddy mess. This muddy mess ended up all over their legs, arms, and face as they continued to swing and play in the mud mixture. My Sister got there in time to see them swing with their legs and arms dragging the ground flipping mud everywhere.

One way to look at this story is to think about our own brilliant idea that turned into a muddy mess. Consider the time, creativity, and effort you put into expressing and acting on the idea only to end with mud on your face, hands, and feet with your efforts going nowhere. You begin to question God with questions like: Wasn't this such a great idea? Why did this happen? Why did my idea fail? A friend and I met for coffee at our local coffee shop and we got to talking and planning an event and the excitement grew. Just as we were taking off with ideas and themes my friend stops us and says let's take some time to pray about this and then we can email our thoughts. I was caught completely off guard as I was in the middle of my own creative consciousness…how was God going to play a part in this, I thought. But she was exactly right. We needed to step back and give God the creative freedom to take our project and bless it, construct it, and guide it.

> *I can do everything through him who gives me strength.*
> *Philippians 4:13*

Promises – Sanctus Real

Sometimes it's hard to keep believing in what you can't see, that everything happens for a reason even the worst life brings, if you're reaching for an answer and you don't know what to pray, just open up the pages let is word be your strength, and hold on to the promises, hold on to the promises.

Life is difficult and everyone has struggles. Everyone has fears, or regrets, or crushed dreams. In the midst of the storm and even after the storm it can be difficult to see the goodness of God and all the ways His love surrounds us. Through my own diagnosis of autoimmune lung disease and the resulting losses; my career, my house, some of my independence, and my financial peace; I have learned that holding on to God's promises means more than the trite (even sometimes hurtful) words which people commonly use to try to encourage you when you are deep in the storm.
It is even something beyond the resolute decision to pull your way through the storm with your own might. It is the resolute decision to believe in a sovereign God. We can better understand the word/subject/action of sovereign by recalling a few of its synonyms; ruler, monarch, absolute, reigning, leading, uppermost, and paramount. God's goodness, God's favor is the gift of himself. The good thing as noted in the verse below is we have a God, the ruler, an absolute leader, whose paramount concern is for us. He wants to sit with his in our times of anxiety and stress. He want to rejoice with us in our celebrations and happiness.

For the Lord God is a sun and shield; the Lord bestows favor and honor; no good thing does he withhold from those whose walk is blameless. Psalm 84:11

Where I Belong – Building 429

> *So when the walls come falling down on me, and when I'm lost in the current of a raging sea, I have this blessed assurance holding me, All I know is I am not home yet, this is not where I belong, take this world and give me Jesus, this is not where I belong.*

I for one am thankful we are not destined to make earth and all the problems of an earthly life our future forever. As Christ's followers and those who have accepted him as our personal savior and turned from the sin that so easily entangles we have a treasure stored up in heaven. This song by Building 429 captures the struggle of life on earth but the hope we have in a future home in heaven.

What a sweet picture we have in the verse for today. The Lamb, Jesus Christ, our Savior, the one who bore our sins on the cross is a shepherd. He is leading us home. God, our father, is there to wipe our tears and welcome us. What joy there will be, when my savior I will see. This scene makes me think of my nephew and the day he showed up at Papa's house unannounced and unaccompanied. He burst through the garage door, stomped in, and asked Papa what was going on. Luckily Papa's house is just around the corner from his house but nonetheless for a four year old the trek alone was a long one. Papa asked him if he walked over by himself and Cooper answered with, "No, I ran here." I want that to be my answer when I am called home to heaven…did you walk here dear child; "No, I ran here!"

> *For the Lamb at the center of the throne will be their shepherd; he will lead them to springs of living water. And God will wipe away every tear from their eyes.*
> **Revelation 7:17**

10,000 Reasons (Bless the Lord) – Matt Redman

You're rich in love, slow to anger, your name is great and your heart is kind for all your goodness I will keep on singing, 10,000 reasons for my heart to find. To Bless the Lord oh my soul, oh my soul worship his holy name sing like never before oh my soul I worship your holy name, and on that day when my strength is failing, the end draws near and my time has come still my soul will sing your praise unending, 10,000 years and then forevermore.

My Sister, Jessica, and I run a business for eight weeks in the summer teaching swimming lessons to children of all ages. Each Spring we hire our staff, start the enrollment process, and gear up for eight week of intense focus and time commitment. Jessica is almost giddy by the time swim season rolls around. Her passion for teaching and enjoyment of swimming show as she answers enrollment questions, leads the staff, and teaches classes. For most of the thirty-two days of actual teaching lessons she could easily come up with 100 reasons why she loves the program, enjoys teaching swimming lessons, loves working with the staff, likes fielding questions, and delights in being a leader/pool manager. She enjoys working at the pool so much she might even be able to come up with 200 reasons why she loves her summer job. I am guessing each of us have some kind of activity or person or people in which a list of why we love it or them would be pretty easy to start. Imagine though being asked to create a list of the top 10,000 reasons why you love your job or why you love your family. A bit overwhelming! Sure! Impossible…many would think so! Incredibly amazing that we can find 10,000 reasons to bless the Lord no matter what our current set of circumstances and yet we only need one, his death on a cross, to find the hope for the next 10,000 years.

> *Ascribe to the Lord the glory due his name. Bring an offering and come before him; worship the Lord in the splendor due his holiness. I Chronicles 16:29*

OUR GOD – CHRIS TOMLIN

Our God is greater, our God is stronger, God you are higher than any other, our God is Healer, awesome in power our God our God. Into the darkness you shine, out of the ashes we rise. There's no one like you, none like you.

My nephew Cooper (age four) decided he was going to get all dressed up in his three piece suit. After some time of working on this task he entered his Mom's (my Sister) room. He said, "Mom, Mom, Mom… I need a little help here." When my Sister really looked at him he had the vest on the outside of the suit coat and was having trouble getting it buttoned. He had worked and worked to get dressed on his own until the frustration was at an overwhelming level and he knew he needed help. So he went to the source. The one he knew could fix it.

Why is it we sometimes work and work at something when all we really need to do it take it to the one who can fix it? "Heavenly Father, Heavenly Father, Heavenly Father…I need a little help here," can be our battle cry as we face the struggles of daily life on Earth. Just as Cooper was confident his Mother could not only understand his troubles and frustration but could solve the problem. We too are assured of God's understanding, love, and ability to problem solve for us in any situation.

I lift up my eyes to the hill- where does my help come from? My help comes from the Lord, the Maker of heaven and earth. Psalm 121:1-2

Lay down my Life – Sidewalk Prophets

All your pain will be made mine, all your troubles, the tears you cry, give it up all that binds, I will place it on my shoulders and up this hill I'll climb, father give me strength, I know there is no other way, so I lay down my life for you, this is the moment when all will be made new, I know that you don't understand, this is part of a greater plan, this is love that had to bleed to bring you mercy, to set you free, you are mine and I am yours.

I was reading an article about the brain, brain development, and different patterns of the brain in the way we think, act, and learn. It was part of my preparation for a class I taught each summer called the brain compatible classroom. A section of the article discussed moral development in the brain and posed this scenario; What would you do if all you had to do was flip a switch and you would save either a train full of strangers or your loved one? There was no way to save both, it had to be the train packed with people who mean nothing to you or your loved one whom you share a bond with. Which would you save?

Essentially this was the choice God was looking at when deciding to have Jesus, his only son, perfect and blameless, die on a cross for the world. For our sin and shame. God looked at his dilemma and choose us. Jesus suffered a horrible death on the cross so that we may live.

For God so loved the world, that He gave his only son that whoever believes in him shall not perish but have eternal life. John 3:16

Lift Me Up – The Afters

You know my heart is heavy and the hurt is deep, when I feel like giving up you're reminding me that we all fall down sometimes, when I hit the ground you lift me up when I am weak, your arms wrap around me, your love catches me so I'm letting go, you lift me up when I can't see, your heart is all I need, your love carries me so I'm letting go.

In September of 2013 I had surgery to repair a chest wall hernia. The hernia was in the muscle directly under the previous lung biopsy/Thoracotomy scar on the right side. It caused extreme levels of stabbing pain when I would take a breath after lifting or moving something or after working out. The lung would actually balloon out into the space created by the hole in the muscle and chest wall tissue. As all surgeons do, Dr. Miller down played the details of the surgery and it was not until I woke up in recovery with a chest tube that it dawned on me I had just had another major lung surgery. This time, however, there was no epidural to mask the pain of a chest tube. The first twenty-four hours with the chest tube were miserable. It was uncomfortable, painful when breathing, and almost unbearable when trying to move around. Just when I thought I was at my wits end and there was no way I could stand this another minute in walked Dr. Miller to remove the chest tube. In my urgency to get the tube out I flung open my hospital gown, rolled to the side, and told Dr. Miller I was happy to see him. It didn't matter to me who was in the room or what they saw I just wanted that tube out of my chest. However, Dr. Miller gave my host of encouragers a minute to exit the room and then he proceeded with removing the chest tube. Just when I thought I couldn't take having that tube inside my chest for one more second much less a minute for people to leave and him to prepare, I made it because the end of the pain, the end of suffering, and the end of the uncomfortableness was in sight. Dr. Miller was in my room, he had the tools and he was preparing to solve my most pressing problem. In so many ways that is exactly what God is trying to do for us. He enters the space, he comes in time for the rescue, he opens our heart to a healing of a different sort. We can find strength in knowing he has arrived, he is here with us in our pain, in our suffering and in our uncomfortableness. Always able and always willing to lift us up!

> ***God is our refuge and strength, an ever-present help in times of trouble. Psalm 46:1***

Redeemed – Big Daddy Weave

Seems like all I could see was struggle, haunted by ghosts that lived in my past, bound up in shackles of all my failures, wondering how long is this going to last, then you look at this prisoner and say to me son stop fighting a fight that's already been won, I am redeemed, you set me free, so I shake off these heavy chains and wipe away every stain, I'm not who I used to be, I am redeemed, I'm redeemed.

My nephew Cooper enjoys dressing up and acting as if he is different action heroes. His costumes include Captain America, Batman, Superman, Ironman, and the Hulk. Cooper's actions and even his voice tend to take on the characteristics of the super hero he is pretending to be. It is quite a sight to watch this five year old redhead bound into the living room yelling, "Hulk SMASH."

Somewhat similar to Cooper when I was diagnosed with an autoimmune lung disease I took on the characteristics and perception of a person with a serious illness. As the disease and treatment side effects progressed it became clear that I was in for some major life changes. All I could see was the struggle and sometimes it is still all I see until I remind myself or someone else reminds me that I am a child of the King. I am redeemed. I get to take on the characteristics of the redeemed. I have help in the struggle.

He redeemed us in order that the blessing given to Abraham might come to the Gentiles through Christ Jesus, so that by faith we might receive the promise of the Spirit. Galatians 3:14

Only A Mountain – Jason Castro

Another day another fight, it always feels like an uphill climb, another step another mile, the story of your life, it's harder than you ever thought, and it costs you everything you've got, when your back against the wall, and you feel like giving up, this is only a mountain, you don't have to find your way around it, tell it to move, it'll move, tell to fall, it'll fall, this is only a moment, you don't have to let your fear control it, tell to move, it will move, tell it to fall, it will fall.

I used to really struggle with songs and bible verses like these. I would get rather frustrated because sometimes no matter how much faith we have and no matter how much trust we devote or how much time we spend in prayer sometimes things just don't work out. Bad things happen! And bad things sometimes continue to happen. I have learned something important through my illness journey with all the negative changes, side effects, and upheaval; the mountain does not pertain to my illness, or even the changes which occur because of the disease but instead it is referring to the inner world of chaos which in a crisis situation can seem like a mountain in my path. Making life feel overwhelming, difficult, and placing additional hardship in an already difficult path.

We could think about ourselves as the mountain blocking the way to hope. While God is still in the business of big miracles and He still moves mountains often the miracle is that we function and contribute to life through the hardship, difficulty or mountain experience. Living life in the midst of hardship and being able to make a difference is like the miracle of moving mountains.

I tell you the truth, if you have faith as small as a mustard seed, you can say to this mountain, move from here to there and it will move. Nothing will be impossible for you. Matthew 17:20

Overcomer – Mandisa

Got so much on your mind, nothing's really going right, looking for a ray of hope, whatever it is you may be going through, I know He's not going to let it get the best of you, You're an overcomer, stay in the fight until the final round, you're not going under, cause God is holding you right now, you might be down for a moment, feeling like it's hopeless, that's when he reminds you, you're an overcomer.

When my niece, Kenzie, was three she was misdiagnosed with Type 1 Diabetes. Kenzie was immediately admitted to our local children's hospital and my Sister and Brother-in-law were quickly introduced to the world of parenting a diabetic child. There were finger pricks, protein and sugar calorie counting, and insulin shots. They learned about danger signs, the equipment needed, and local support groups. When they returned home they began their new routine of checking blood sugar levels, watching what she ate, and giving insulin accordingly. One morning, during this regular routine, my Sister tried to prick Kenzie's middle finger to test but after squeezing it nothing came out. Then Kenzie held up her pointer finger from the other hand and told her mom, "That one must be empty, try this one."

This could have been a miraculous healing or she never really had diabetes to begin with because they got to where they could not give her any insulin or she would get to low of blood sugar levels and when they tested on a regular basis she was in the normal range without any medications. She will still talk about her experiences on occasions but mostly those uncertain and scary times with diabetes have past.

Unfortunately for many people, including myself, the miraculous healing has not come and we are faced with the day to day problems, fears, and disappointments associated with a chronic illness. That does not mean, however, that we must give in to the uncertainty, anxiety, and the fears connected with living with a chronic illness or chronic pain. As Mandisa says in her song *Overcomer*, "we may be down for a moment feeling hopeless but God is not going to let it get the best of us." We may not get the physical healing to overcome the disease process but we can have a mental and emotional victory to overcome the trials and fears which so entangle our hearts and minds during a health challenge or any challenging event in our lives for that matter.

> *I have told you these things, so that in me you may have peace. In this world you will have trouble. But take heart! I have overcome the world. John 16:33*

Get Down – Audio Adrenaline

All I need is another day where I can't seem to get away from the little things that drag me down, I'm sure you've had a day like me where nothing seems to set you free from the burdens you can't carry on your own, in your weakness he is stronger, in your darkness he shines through, when your crying he's your comfort, when you're all alone he's carrying you, I get down, he lifts me up, I get down he lifts me up.

Have you ever had one of those days where everything seems to be going wrong and it is only 7:00am? The kids won't get out of bed, the alarm didn't go off, you forgot to wash your favorite pair of pants, the shower water took forever to get warm, and the toast is burnt.

My morning like the one previously described began with the snooze button, a long shower, trouble finding the right outfit, and breakfast on the run. As I was headed north on highway 7, I thought the twenty-five minute drive would be good to clear my head and refocus my flustered mind in order to prepare for a full day of teaching science and coaching volleyball. Instead, it was about seven minutes into the drive when I heard a loud explosion then my car began shaking and swerving. I completely lost control of the car and spun several times before ending in a ditch on the side of the road.

I was shaken but thankfully not hurt. Knowing my Mom was just about ready to leave, I called her to ask if she could come pick me up. I opened the car door only to find at least a foot of mud waiting for me on the outside. As I stepped down, my foot, with dress shoe, sunk deep into the watery, smelly, muddy mess. My shoe suction cupped to the bottom and completely came off when I tried lifting my foot to take a step. I retrieved my shoe, threw it to the open, dry ground and continued my trek to the trunk where I had stored my school bag. My little red, two door Honda Civic had to be pulled out of the muddy mess by a tow truck.

We are fortunate to have a God who will act as our tow truck. Pulling us out of the muddy mess we find ourselves in. He gives us a place of sure footing and trust. Whether it is a messy situation like health concerns, broken relationships, financial struggles or personally with emotional distress, spiritual fears, and mental anxiety; God is with us hearing our cry.

> *I waited patiently for the Lord; he turned to me and heard my cry. He lifted me out of the slimy pit, out of the mud and mire; he set my feet on a rock and gave me a firm place to stand. Psalm 40:1-2*

Through It All – Selah

I've had many tears and sorrows, I've had questions for tomorrow, there have been times I didn't know right from wrong, but in every situation God gave blessed consolation that my trials only come to make me strong, and it was through it all, through it all, I've learned to trust in Jesus, I've learned to trust in God, through it all, through it all I've learned to depend upon his word.

In my illness journey with an autoimmune lung disease I have had many moments of sadness, tears, questions, and trials. Recently, I was faced with a situation in making a choice to remain on a daily medication called Cellcept or return to a daily chemotherapy drug called Imuran. Both medications presented negative consequences and during this journey I have been on both of them at one time or another. Still I struggled greatly in making a decision and then feeling good about the choice I made. I looked to my family for understanding and approval. As I transitioned to the Imuran from the Cellcept and experienced a few of the negative side effects of taking a daily chemotherapy drug, such as fatigue and nausea, I truly began to question my choice. I wondered and even debated with myself if I had made the right choice. It was during the spiral of self-doubt, worry, and stress that my dear friend, and adopted mother, Jan wrote me a note that said she didn't think there was a right answer…that it seemed more like weighing the pros and cons of two not so good choices. Sometimes our journey will take us to a place of nothing but negative choices and dismal looking future scenarios but it is in these times that we must strive to trust in God.

As the song says "Through it all, through it all, I've learned to trust in Jesus, I've learned to trust in God, I've learned to depend upon his word." I am in awe of the author of this song, who seems to be at such a peaceful, reflective place in life. Having the ability to write the song using the past tense of learn. Showing a final destination…learned. I think I would have used the term learning as in always striving to do better and to accomplish more knowledge and understanding. Through it all I am learning to trust in Jesus seems a little more appropriate for my journey as I travel the path of having a chronic illness.

The fact that I am still learning helps me understand the deeper meaning of scripture verses such as that one below. On the surface many of us could argue with the printed meaning. Delight yourself in the Lord and he will give you the desires of your heart… This verse presents a conflict when you feel you have a devoted, prayerful life to God and yet nothing good seems to happen in the desires or dreams of you heart. For me I could name disappointments in things like not having married, no children of my own, my Mother passed away, being diagnosed with an autoimmune lung disease, not being able to work, having to sell my house, and not getting to use my doctorate degree to find an administrative position in education. All have been or are the desires of my heart so why have they not happened? I guess there are several possible answers but I believe God is talking in a bigger picture about our ultimate desire to be loved and to have peace. A peace not offered in our frail and broken world but only a love and peace which God can supply.

> *Trust in the Lord and do good; dwell in the land and enjoy safe pasture. Delight yourself in the Lord and he will give you the desires of your heart. Psalm 37:3-4*

Healing Begins – Tenth Avenue North

So you thought you had to keep this up, all the work that you do so we think that you're good and you can't believe it is not enough, all the walls you build up are just glass on the outside, so let them fall down, there's freedom waiting in the sound, this is where the healing begins, this is where the healing starts, when you come to where you are broken within, this is where the light meets the dark, the light meets the dark.

  This entry to my CaringBridge site was written on December 24, 2013. Merry Christmas to all my caringbridge site readers. I cherish each and every one of you. I feel privileged to have the opportunity to share my journey with you both the ups and downs and the good and the bad. Isn't that really what life is about…doing life with others through the good and the bad. In this holiday season I feel so blessed to have such an amazing support system and what a blessing you all have been in my life over this past year as well as the years since my diagnosis. Many people take the time at Christmas and write to others about their year, their joys, vacations, and accomplishments. I wish with my entire being that I could write about an expedition on a sunny beach somewhere or my most recent accomplishment as a school administrator instead God has me placed right in the palm of His hand. Using me to mentor a new middle schooler, cheer on my favorite soccer player, laugh at the cutest red-head, five year old, listen to the four year old, and hold the new baby boy. Not to mention spending time with my Sister, who just happens to be my best friend. I have enjoyed Wednesday morning bible study with new friends and an opportunity to volunteer at Santa Fe Trail Middle School helping Kayla's academic teacher team with team activities. I can't say I have adjusted to life with an autoimmune lung disease and a constant migraine headache but I can say that with your support and my faith in a loving, heavenly father, who has an ultimate plan, I am learning to have moments of peace and joy...two areas which are quite important to making the Christmas Season special. May this 2013 Christmas season be filled with peace and joy as you celebrate with friends and family the difference God made for us in sending His son as our savior and Lord.

> *Do not be anxious about anything, but in everything through prayer and petition with thanksgiving present your requests to God. And the peace of God, which transcends all understanding, will guard your hearts and your minds in Christ Jesus. Philippians 4:6-7*

SPEAK LIFE – TOBYMAC

Some days life feels perfect other days it just ain't working, the good, the bad, the right, the wrong and everything in between, we can turn a heart with the words we say, speak life, speak life, through the deadest darkest night, speak life, speak life, when the sun won't shine and you don't know why, look into the eyes of the brokenhearted watch them come alive as soon as you speak hope, you speak love, you speak life, speak Life.

 I spent three and a half days in the Behavioral Health Services floor at one of our local hospitals following a medication interactions that caused Serotonin Syndrome. This syndrome caused increased amounts of anxiety, racing feelings, random suicidal thoughts, and difficulty concentrating. Physical symptoms like heart palpitations, sweating, entire body shakiness, and an intense heartburn sensation in my chest and stomach also accompanied the serotonin syndrome. Due to my autoimmune disease, Sjogren's Syndrome, I already experience terrible, daily migraine type headaches but these headaches have been magnified with the increase in serotonin during this experience. One day my head was hurting so badly and the nurse was hesitant to give me some medication that I said if we don't get meds here you might as well take me downstairs to the ER because something is going to have to happen to help this. I got the meds and rested till the headache's intensity reduced a little.
 Many of my fellow patients were depressed and suicidal. Many also were dealing with chronic illnesses, like myself. As I began to feel a little better as the effects of the overload of serotonin began to wear off, I noticed even more similarities between everyone on the floor. My roommate, a woman close to my age felt the world would be better off if she killed herself and donated her organs to people who have a life, family, friends, something worth living for. She was an amazing artist, kind-hearted, and was dealing with health issues in addition to past trauma and mental health concerns. I thought about the story she would have to tell if she could only

realize her worth through Jesus Christ. Prior to being discharged from the 6th floor I had the opportunity to speak life, speak hope to my roommate. I asked her if I could share a few things I believe about our Lord and Savior Jesus Christ. With tears streaming down her face I share about Jesus's death on the cross for us and our sins and his resurrection giving us a new life in Him, finding worth in Him, a source of strength through Him. I felt led by the Holy Spirit to ask her if she had a Bible of her own which she could read. When she answered she thought there was one in the break room I got mine out of my bag and handed it to her. I said it is written all over, highlighted, underlined and dated but it is yours now. As her tears were flowing she managed to say thank you, no one has ever cared like this. I told her Jesus cares like this every moment of every day, and you are his child, He loves you. I finished with a prayer for both of us, we exchanged phone numbers and she gave me one of her artwork pieces.

As I walked out of that room I had a smile on my face not because I was leaving what was probably the second most horrible time in my life but because God gave me, a broken, anxious-filled, illness ridden, Marlena, a chance to speak life and speak hope, and watch the eyes of the brokenhearted come alive through the words of the Holy Spirit verbalized through me. What amazing opportunities await us and through our circumstances!

> *May the words of my mouth and the meditation of my heart be pleasing in your sight, O LORD, my ROCK and my Redeemer. Psalm 19:14*

BLESSINGS – LAURA STORY

We pray for blessings, we pray for peace, comfort for family, protection while we sleep, we pray for healing, we pray for your mighty hand to ease our suffering, all the while you hear each spoken need, what if your blessing come through raindrops, what if your healing comes through tears, what if a thousand sleepless nights are what it takes to know you're near, what if trials of this life are your mercies in disguise.

Author, bible study guru, and speaker, Beth Moore, once said in a video that a boring life is not much of a story. She went on to demonstrate how most of us would choose books based on conflict, trials, and problems versus the one about cleaning the bathroom or my work in the garden. This song speaks to the very heart of this issue. Trials, tears, and rough situations have a way of turning out as blessings from the Lord. Below I have used each letter of the word BLESSINGS to record something or someone who blesses my life in two categories. One category which is easy to find the blessing and the other not so easy to feel blessed.

Easy to See Blessings	More Difficult to See the Blessings
Brothers	**B**ad headaches
Loving Parents	**L**abs Tests
Easter	**E**motional stress
Sisters	**S**jogren's Syndrome- autoimmune disease
Sporting KC Soccer	**S**urgeries
Invitations	**I**muran – daily chemotherapy drug
Nieces and Nephews	**N**on Specific Interstitial Pneumonitis- Lung Disease
Grilled out Food	**G**reat doctors
Soccer	**S**tays at the hospital

However, it is both categories of blessing which compose my testimony to the faithfulness of a loving heavenly father who blesses us beyond measure even when we do not see or feel it. It is easy to get lost in the burdens and heaviness of the more difficult side to see the blessings but our verse for today reminds us to stay strong and courageous, to know the ultimate blessing from God is His presence with us all the time, through the good and the bad, through peace and the storm, through hanging out with family at a backyard picnic or hanging out in the hospital room... GOD does it with us!

> *Be strong and courageous. Do not be afraid or terrified because of them, for the LORD your God goes with you; he will never leave you nor forsake you. Deuteronomy 31:6*

DEAD MAN WALKING
- JEREMY CAMP

Then you rescued me and now I can breathe. I was a Dead man walking until I was a man walking with you. I was a blind man falling until I felt the life you're calling me to. I was a Dead man walking until you Loved this Dead man walking back to Life.

    Being Loved makes all the difference in giving us purpose, life, and freedom. As dead men walking we understand the weight of sin in our lives and the shame that the sin can fill our soul. This soul shame makes us lose our focus on living for God and being an instrument through which God can accomplish His plan.

    Putting our trust and hope in the Lord our God helps us to refocus in order to restore a right relationship with our God; therefore being a conduit for living out the purpose God has for each of us. My nephew Cooper demonstrated this concept as he and a friend were playing around the yard and ran into the neighbors backyard. That house happened to be empty at this time. Cooper and his friend looked in the house and opened the back door. They entered the house and proceeded to look around and then just ran out and finished they games. Cooper was inside his own house for a while, when he came up to his Mom and said "Mom I need to tell you something. He then said that his friend and himself went into the house which was breaking and entering a property which was not his own." He was worried the police would come. He had to confess his shame and guilt in order to move forward. I am still amazed at how many lessons we can learn from the children in our lives.

Why am I discouraged? Why is my heart so sad? I will put my hope in God - my Savior. Psalms 42:5

THE CHAMPION - CARRIE UNDERWOOD

I am the Champion, I am invincible, unbreakable, unstoppable, unshakable. They knock me down I get up again. I was made for this. I was born to win.

My niece Kenzie is a competitive soccer player. She really has been playing since age 2 when she would get out there with her Sister's recreational team and run around pushing people to get the ball, or yelling at the players to give her the ball, and best of all was when she would be over by the parents chatting it up with the sideline. Our church league was a good start for her but we quickly noted what a very aggressive, naturally gifted, and hard working player she was on the field. My Sister and Brother-in -Law decided to have her try-out for one of our local competitive soccer club called TOCA FC. TOCA's emphasis on faith, family, futball (soccer) and their focus on developing players with incredible foot skills was a major draw to their program.

Kenzie has this song ***The Champion*** on her pregame playlist. The playlist is a collection of songs which motivate her to do her best at the game. These songs pump her up to give her best effort and to remember if she gets knock down or loses the ball to get right back up. She truly has become a leader in hard work and giving you best effort on the field. This mirrors the effort we should be giving to living our christian life out in front of others. It's not that we are perfect all the time, it's not that we don't fall down but because of Christ our champion over sin and death we can get back up and keep focused on winning in life.

> ***We do this by keeping our eyes on Jesus, the champion who initiates and perfects our faith. Because of the joy awaiting Him, He endured the cross, disregarding its shame. Now He is seated in the place of honor beside God's throne. Hebrews 12:2.***

I'M GONNA LET IT GO - JASON GRAY

It's hard for me to let go, hard for me to breathe, thinking that I gotta control it all. I can feel my worry and anxiety. I can feel my heart go boom boom boom.

My Brother David and his son (my nephew) Henry went on a bike ride and crashed. (Not into each other-they both went down on a wooden bridge not far from our house. It was very slippery from the rain.) According to Henry he was able to save himself with a cartwheel, somersault and barrel roll. David wasn't so fancy and he broke his right arm. David was in a sling and they had an appointment to see a specialist. This is the unknown territory when we cannot control life. Questions were spinning around. Would he need surgery? How would he work not being able to use his right arm? How long would he be in the sling? Would he need physical therapy? And the heart goes boom boom boom. It is so easy to spin out of control when we forget we have help through trouble when we can be patient and have an attitude of prayer.

Rejoice in our confident hope. Be patient in trouble, and keep on praying. Romans 12:12

Scars - I Am They

Look back from the other side, I can see now with open eyes, darkest water and deepest pain. I wouldn't trade it for anything 'cause my brokenness brought me to You and these wounds are a story you'll use. So I'm thankful for the scars.

When I had surgery to place the neuro-stimulator, the operating team shave just about an inch of hair from above my ear to the bottom of my neck. They did the surgery which included the opening the skin just behind my ear. Also during this procedure there is a very small scar made on my forehead just about at my hairline, which remember at the time was shaved. The largest scar is on my chest where the battery and control piece is just under my skin.

I took Kayla to drivers education class not long after having this procedure completed. The surgical area behind my ear was still covered with bandages and tape. I got Kayla settled got back in line to pay for the class and a man standing a couple people behind me said to me, "Nice haircut… bringing back the 80's." I choose not to respond and no one else made a peep so I paid, signed the paperwork, and headed out. All the time wondering how the dude missed the bandages behind my ear.

"For I know the plans I have for you," says the Lord. "They are plans for good and not for disaster, to give you a future and a hope." Jeremiah 29:11

Hope In Front of Me - Danny Gokey

I've been running through rain that I thought would never end. Try to Make it on faith but I struggle against the wind. I've seen the dark and the broken places but I know in my soul however bad it gets, I'll be alright. There's hope in front of me, there's a light I still see it.

Sometimes life seems like the journey is only dark, lonely, and full of broken places. We combat on all sides of life temptations, lost dreams, unhappy people, death, overburdened responsibilities and frustrations of all kinds which seems to zap not only our energy for life but also the enjoyment of life is lost in the mix. Consider the example of making a cake. When you start with the flour mix there is nothing in that bowl of much value. You would not serve the flour mixture to your family as a cake. Therefore you begin to add other key ingredients to bring your cake to a yummy dessert. Finding hope in life is like using all the ingredients to make a cake. Some of those ingredients you know what they do for the end product but really none of them individually taste that good. This is a metaphor for finding the hope in front of us. Keeping our eyes on Jesus. Letting God add the ingredients to our lives the good, bad, happy, sad, enjoyable, frustrating, peaceful, and stormy. Keeping our heart locked in on seeing the glimmer of light in front of us and knowing we have surrendered our life to the hope in Jesus can help us meditate on the things of God rather than the defeating things of this earth.

> ***And this hope will not lead to disappointment. For we know how dearly God loves us, because he has given us the Holy Spirit to fill our hearts with his love. Romans 5:5***

Joy - For King and Country

Can't seem to find the rhythm, Just want to sing the blues, Feels like a song that never....Stops. Gotta get that Fire Fire back in my bones, before my heart heart turns into stone, oh hear my prayer tonight. I choose Joy.

My niece Kenzie and I went to the Independence, MO. SPCA to find me a new dog. It had been some time since Tucker, my Jack Russel, died and I was ready for a new pup. We had a couple dogs on our list to check out since we had done some homework on the dogs housed at the shelter. One in particular caught our eye. She is a Staffordshire Terrier Pit Bull, tanish, orange in color, big dog. As soon as she came through the door to the outside play area she came straight over to me and gave my hands big licks of kisses. Then when Kenzie was playing with her. Kenzie through the ball and Maggie brought is right back to her. We did not need to see any other dogs. We found the right one.

Maggie brings me so much joy. She makes me smile and even laugh at her funny antics and big dog looking meanness, when she is scared of her own tail sometimes. What I love most about this big girl is when I am crying with pain, sorrow, or saddness she comes and lays her head on my thigh. If a dog can love me that much...how much more am I loved by God. This produces a JOY that only God can supply, which I can choose during any situations. Joy of what God has done for us. Sending His son to die on the cross and be our savor. Choosing JOY is choosing God's way.

> **Guard your heart above all else, for it determines the course of your life. Proverbs 4:23**

In Closing, music has a way of speaking to the heart, soul, and mind like no other medium. Having a playlist or music station of uplifting and encouraging songs has a way of moving an immovable heart, inspiring a grief stricken soul, and challenging a life to be devoted to the things of Christ. The impact of powerful music to motivate a committed walk with the Lord is unmatched. I can't help but put a smile on my face and a beam in my heart to turn on the local Christian radio station only to hear three children ages 12 (18), 9 (15), and 5 (11) belt out the most recent TobyMac lyrics or sing softly and heartfelt with a Jamie Grace song. PRICELESS!

www.ingramcontent.com/pod-product-compliance
Lightning Source LLC
Chambersburg PA
CBHW030332080526
44584CB00012B/826